PENGUIN P

SELEC

BY WILLIA

WILLIAM WORDSWORTH (1770–1850). English poet, best remembered for his devoted love of nature and rejection of secular values.

William Wordsworth was born in 1770 at Cockermouth, Cumbria, the son of an attorney. His parents died when he was still a child, and the losses are recorded in *The Prelude*, his intense and haunting epic poem on childhood. Educated at St John's College, Cambridge, Wordsworth was dissatisfied with the course and took greater pleasure in a walking tour in 1790 of France, the Alps and Italy. He returned to France for a year at the end of 1791, where he fell in love with Annette Vallon, who bore him a daughter. After returning to England, he published his first poems in 1793: *An Evening Walk* and *Descriptive Sketches*, which are conventional, picturesque descriptions of the Alps. His disillusionment with the French Revolution, which he had strongly advocated, is reflected in his verse drama *The Borderers*, composed in 1796–7 and published in 1842. He worked closely with his friend Samuel Taylor Coleridge and together they produced *Lyrical Ballads* (1798), which contains much of Wordsworth's best-known poetry. In 1799 he and his sister Dorothy settled in Dove Cottage, Grasmere, and in 1802 he married Mary Hutchinson, whom he had known since childhood. In the same year he composed 'Resolution and Independence' and began his ode, 'Intimations of Immortality from Recollections of Early Childhood', which both appeared in *Poems in Two Volumes* (1807). He moved to Ambleside in 1813, where he stayed for the rest of his life. At this time his output was prolific, including *The Excursion* (1814), *The White Doe of Rylstone* (1914), *Peter Bell* and *The Waggoner*, both published in 1819, and many prose works. Wordsworth's popularity gradually increased and in 1843 he succeeded Robert Southey as Poet Laureate. He was deeply venerated by writers such as Matthew Arnold and John Stuart Mill. A great innovator in English poetry, William Wordsworth died in 1850.

This collection gathers together his best-loved poems, including 'My Heart Leaps Up', the 'Lucy' poems, 'To a Sky-lark', 'The Solitary Reaper' and 'Lines Composed Above Tintern Abbey'. The fresh lyricism of Wordsworth's verse has a timeless and universal appeal.

PENGUIN POPULAR CLASSICS

SELECTED POEMS

WILLIAM WORDSWORTH

PENGUIN BOOKS

PENGUIN BOOKS

Published by the Penguin Group

Penguin Books Ltd, 80 Strand, London WC2R 0RL, England

Penguin Putnam Inc., 375 Hudson Street, New York, New York 10014, USA

Penguin Books Australia Ltd, Ringwood, Victoria, Australia

Penguin Books Canada Ltd, 10 Alcorn Avenue, Toronto, Ontario, Canada M4V 3B2

Penguin Books India (P) Ltd, 11 Community Centre, Panchsheel Park,
New Delhi – 110 017, India

Penguin Books (NZ) Ltd, Cnr Rosedale and Airborne Roads, Albany, Auckland,
New Zealand

Penguin Books (South Africa) (Pty) Ltd, 24 Sturdee Avenue, Rosebank 2196, South Africa

Penguin Books Ltd, Registered Offices: 80 Strand, London WC2R 0RL, England

www.penguin.com

Published in Penguin Popular Classics 1996

7

Printed in Great Britain by Cox & Wyman Ltd,
Reading, Berkshire

CONTENTS

v

CONTENTS

POEMS REFERRING TO THE
PERIOD OF CHILDHOOD

MY HEART LEAPS UP

MY heart leaps up when I behold
    A rainbow in the sky:
So was it when my life began;
So it is now I am a man;
So be it when I shall grow old,
    Or let me die!
  The Child is father of the Man;
And I could wish my days to be
Bound each to each by natural piety.
  1804.

TO A BUTTERFLY

STAY near me—do not take thy flight!
    A little longer stay in sight!
Much converse do I find in thee,
Historian of my infancy!
Float near me; do not yet depart!
Dead times revive in thee:
Thou bring'st, gay creature as thou art!
A solemn image to my heart,
My father's family!

Oh ! pleasant, pleasant were the days,
The time, when in our childish plays,
My sister Emmeline and I
Together chased the butterfly !
A very hunter did I rush
Upon the prey :—with leaps and springs
I followed on from brake to bush ;
But she, God love her ! feared to brush
The dust from off its wings.
   1801.

THE SPARROW'S NEST

BEHOLD, within the leafy shade,
   Those bright blue eggs together laid !
On me the chance-discovered sight
Gleamed like a vision of delight.
I started—seeming to espy
The home and sheltered bed,
The Sparrow's dwelling, which, hard by
My Father's house, in wet or dry,
My sister Emmeline and I
   Together visited.

She looked at it and seemed to fear it ;
Dreading, tho' wishing, to be near it :
Such heart was in her, being then
A little Prattler among men.
The Blessing of my later years
Was with me when a boy :
She gave me eyes, she gave me ears ;
And humble cares, and delicate fears;
A heart, the fountain of sweet tears ;
   And love, and thought, and joy.
    1801.

LUCY GRAY

OR, SOLITUDE

OFT I had heard of Lucy Gray:
    And, when I crossed the wild,
I chanced to see at break of day
The solitary child.

No mate, no comrade Lucy knew;
She dwelt on a wide moor,
—The sweetest thing that ever grew
Beside a human door!

You yet may spy the fawn at play,
The hare upon the green;
But the sweet face of Lucy Gray
Will never more be seen.

'To-night will be a stormy night—
You to the town must go;
And take a lantern, Child, to light
Your mother through the snow.'

'That, Father! will I gladly do:
'Tis scarcely afternoon—
The minster-clock has just struck two,
And yonder is the moon!'

At this the Father raised his hook,
And snapped a faggot-band;
He plied his work;—and Lucy took
The lantern in her hand.

Not blither is the mountain roe:
With many a wanton stroke
Her feet disperse the powdery snow,
That rises up like smoke.

The storm came on before its time:
She wandered up and down:
And many a hill did Lucy climb;
But never reached the town.

The wretched parents all that night
Went shouting far and wide;
But there was neither sound nor sight
To serve them for a guide

At daybreak on a hill they stood
That overlooked the moor;
And thence they saw the bridge of wood,
A furlong from their door.

They wept—and, turning homeward, cried,
'In heaven we all shall meet!'
—When in the snow the mother spied
The print of Lucy's feet.

Then downwards from the steep hill's edge
They tracked the footmarks small;
And through the broken hawthorn hedge,
And by the long stone wall;

And then an open field they crossed:
The marks were still the same;
They tracked them on, nor ever lost;
And to the bridge they came.

They followed from the snowy bank
Those footmarks, one by one,
Into the middle of the plank;
And further there were none!

—Yet some maintain that to this day
She is a living child;
That you may see sweet Lucy Gray
Upon the lonesome wild.

O'er rough and smooth she trips along,
And never looks behind;
And sings a solitary song
That whistles in the wind.
    1799.

WE ARE SEVEN

A SIMPLE Child,
        That lightly draws its breath,
And feels its life in every limb,
What should it know of death?

I met a little cottage Girl:
She was eight years old, she said;
Her hair was thick with many a curl
That clustered round her head.

She had a rustic, woodland air,
And she was wildly clad;
Her eyes were fair, and very fair;
—Her beauty made me glad.

'Sisters and brothers, little Maid,
How many may you be?'
'How many? Seven in all,' she said,
And wondering look'd at me.

'And where are they? I pray you tell.'
She answered, 'Seven are we;
And two of us at Conway dwell,
And two are gone to sea.

'Two of us in the churchyard lie,
My sister and my brother;
And in the churchyard cottage I
Dwell near them with my mother.'

'You say that two at Conway dwell,
And two are gone to sea,
Yet ye are seven!—I pray you tell,
Sweet Maid, how this may be?'

Then did the little Maid reply,
'Seven boys and girls are we;
Two of us in the churchyard lie,
Beneath the churchyard tree.'

'You run about, my little Maid,
Your limbs they are alive;
If two are in the churchyard laid,
Then ye are only five?'

'Their graves are green, they may be seen,'
The little Maid replied;
'Twelve steps or more from my mother's door,
And they are side by side.

'My stockings there I often knit,
My kerchief there I hem;
And there upon the ground I sit,
And sing a song to them.

'And often after sunset, Sir,
When it is light and fair,
I take my little porringer,
And eat my supper there.

'The first that died was sister Jane;
In bed she moaning lay,
Till God released her of her pain;
And then she went away.

'So in the churchyard she was laid;
And when the grass was dry,
Together round her grave we play'd,
My brother John and I.

'And when the ground was white with snow,
And I could run and slide,
My brother John was forced to go,
And he lies by her side.'

'How many are you, then,' said I,
'If they two are in heaven?'
Quick was the little Maid's reply,
'O Master! we are seven.'

'But they are dead; those two are dead!
Their spirits are in heaven!'
'Twas throwing words away; for still
The little Maid would have her will,
And said, 'Nay, we are seven!'

1798.

THE PET LAMB

A PASTORAL

THE dew was falling fast, the stars began to blink;
    I heard a voice; it said, 'Drink, pretty creature,
       drink!'
And, looking o'er the hedge, before me I espied
A snow-white mountain lamb with a Maiden at its side.

Nor sheep nor kine were near; the lamb was all alone,
And by a slender cord was tethered to a stone;
With one knee on the grass did the little Maiden kneel,
While to that mountain lamb she gave its evening meal.

The lamb, while from her hand he thus his supper
    took,
Seemed to feast with head and ears; and his tail with
    pleasure shook.
'Drink, pretty creature, drink,' she said in such a tone
That I almost received her heart into my own.

'Twas little Barbara Lewthwaite, a child of beauty
    rare!
I watched them with delight; they were a lovely pair.
Now with her empty can, the maiden turn'd away;
But ere ten yards were gone, her footsteps did she
    stay.

Right towards the lamb she looked; and from a shady
    place,
I, unobserved, could see the workings of her face:
If Nature to her tongue could measured numbers
    bring,
Thus, thought I, to her lamb that little Maid might sing:

'What ails thee, young One? what? Why pull so
    at thy cord?
Is it not well with thee? Well both for bed and board?
Thy plot of grass is soft, and green as grass can be;
Rest, little young One, rest; what is't that aileth thee?

'What is it thou wouldst seek? What is wanting to
    thy heart?
Thy limbs, are they not strong? And beautiful thou
    art:
This grass is tender grass; these flowers they have no
    peers;
And that green corn all day is rustling in thy ears!

'If the sun be shining hot, do but stretch thy woollen
    chain,
This beech is standing by, its covert thou canst gain;
For rain and mountain storms! the like thou need'st
    not fear;
The rain and storm are things that scarcely can come
    here.

'Rest, little young One, rest; thou hast forgot the day
When my father found thee first in places far away:
Many flocks were on the hills, but thou wert own'd
    by none;
And thy mother from thy side for evermore was gone.

'He took thee in his arms, and in pity brought thee
    home:
A blessed day for thee! then whither wouldst thou
    roam?
A faithful nurse thou hast; the dam that did thee
    yean
Upon the mountain-tops no kinder could have been.

'Thou know'st that twice a day I have brought thee
    in this can
Fresh water from the brook, as clear as ever ran;
And twice in the day, when the ground is wet with
    dew,
I bring thee draughts of milk, warm milk it is, and
    new.

'Thy limbs will shortly be twice as stout as they are
    now,
Then I'll yoke thee to my cart like a pony in the
    plough;
My playmate thou shalt be; and when the wind is
    cold,
Our hearth shall be thy bed, our house shall be thy
    fold.

'It will not, will not rest!—Poor creature, can it be
That 'tis thy mother's heart which is working so in
    thee?
Things that I know not of belike to thee are dear,
And dreams of things which thou canst neither see
    nor hear.

'Alas, the mountain-tops that look so green and fair!
I've heard of fearful winds and darkness that come
    there;
The little brooks that seem all pastime and all play,
When they are angry, roar like lions for their prey.

'Here thou need'st not dread the raven in the sky;
Night and day thou art safe,—our cottage is hard by.
Why bleat so after me? Why pull so at thy chain?
Sleep—and at break of day I will come to thee
    again!'

As homeward through the lane I went with lazy
    feet,
This song to myself did I oftentimes repeat ;
And it seemed, as I retraced the ballad line by line,
That but half of it was hers, and one half of it was
    mine.

Again, and once again did I repeat the song ;
' Nay,' said I, ' more than half to the damsel must
    belong,
For she looked with such a look, and she spake with
    such a tone,
That I almost received her heart into my own.'

   1800.

INFLUENCE OF NATURAL OBJECTS

IN CALLING FORTH AND STRENGTHENING THE IMAGI-
NATION IN BOYHOOD AND EARLY YOUTH

WISDOM and Spirit of the universe !
    Thou Soul that art the Eternity of thought !
And giv'st to forms and images a breath
And everlasting motion ! not in vain,
By day or star light, thus from my first dawn
Of childhood didst thou intertwine for me
The passions that build up our human soul,
Not with the mean and vulgar works of Man ;
But with high objects, with enduring things,
With life and nature ; purifying thus
The elements of feeling and of thought.

And sanctifying by such discipline
Both pain and fear, until we recognise
A grandeur in the beatings of the heart.

Nor was this fellowship vouchsafed to me
With stinted kindness.   In November days,
When vapours, rolling down the valleys, made
A lonely scene more lonesome ; among woods
At noon ; and 'mid the calm of summer nights,
When, by the margin of the trembling lake,
Beneath the gloomy hills, homeward I went
In solitude, such intercourse was mine :
Mine was it in the fields both day and night,
And by the waters all the summer long.

   And in the frosty season, when the sun
Was set, and, visible for many a mile,
The cottage windows through the twilight blazed,
I heeded not the summons : happy time
It was indeed for all of us ; for me
It was a time of rapture !   Clear and loud
The village clock toll'd six—I wheel'd about,
Proud and exulting, like an untired horse
That cares not for his home.—All shod with steel,
We hissed along the polished ice, in games
Confederate, imitative of the chase
And woodland pleasures,—the resounding horn,
The pack loud-chiming, and the hunted hare.
So through the darkness and the cold we flew,
And not a voice was idle : with the din
Smitten, the precipices rang aloud ;
The leafless trees and every icy crag
Tinkled like iron ; while far-distant hills

Into the tumult sent an alien sound
Of melancholy, not unnoticed while the stars,
Eastward, were sparkling clear, and in the west
The orange sky of evening died away.

Not seldom from the uproar I retired
Into a silent bay, or sportively
Glanced sideway, leaving the tumultuous throng,
To cut across the reflex of a star;
Image, that, flying still before me, gleamed
Upon the glassy plain : and oftentimes,
When we had given our bodies to the wind,
And all the shadowy banks on either side
Came sweeping through the darkness, spinning still
The rapid line of motion, then at once
Have I, reclining back upon my heels,
Stopped short; yet still the solitary cliffs
Wheeled by me—even as if the earth had rolled
With visible motion her diurnal round !
Behind me did they stretch in solemn train,
Feebler and feebler, and I stood and watched
Till all was tranquil as a summer sea.

1799.

POEMS FOUNDED ON THE
AFFECTIONS

THE BROTHERS

'THESE Tourists, Heaven preserve us! needs
    must live
A profitable life : some glance along,
Rapid and gay, as if the earth were air,
And they were butterflies to wheel about
Long as the summer lasted : some, as wise,
Perched on the forehead of a jutting crag,
Pencil in hand and book upon the knee,
Will look and scribble, scribble on and look,
Until a man might travel twelve stout miles,
Or reap an acre of his neighbour's corn.
But for that moping Son of Idleness—
Why can he tarry *yonder ?*—In our churchyard
Is neither epitaph nor monument,
Tombstone nor name—only the turf we tread
And a few natural graves.'

                    To Jane, his wife,
Thus spake the homely Priest of Ennerdale.
It was a July evening ; and he sate
Upon the long stone seat beneath the eaves
Of his old cottage,—as it chanced, that day,

Employed in winter's work.   Upon the stone
His wife sate near him, teasing matted wool,
While, from the twin cards, toothed with glittering
        wire,
He fed the spindle of his youngest child,
Who, in the open air, with due accord
Of busy hands and back-and-forward steps,
Her large round wheel was turning.   Towards the
        field
In which the Parish Chapel stood alone,
Girt round with a bare ring of mossy wall,
While half-an-hour went by, the Priest had sent
Many a long look of wonder ; and at last,
Risen from his seat, beside the snow-white ridge
Of carded wool which the old man had piled,
He laid his implements with gentle care,
Each in the other lock'd ; and down the path
That from his cottage to the churchyard led,
He took his way, impatient to accost
The Stranger, whom he saw still lingering there.

'Twas one well known to him in former days,
A Shepherd-lad ; who ere his sixteenth year
Had left that calling, tempted to intrust
His expectations to the fickle winds
And perilous waters ; with the mariners
A fellow-mariner ;—and so had fared
Through twenty seasons ; but he had been reared
Among the mountains, and he in his heart
Was half a shepherd on the stormy seas.
Oft in the piping shrouds had Leonard heard
The tones of waterfalls, and inland sounds
Of caves and trees :—and, when the regular wind

Between the tropics filled the steady sail,
And blew with the same breath through days and
    weeks,
Lengthening invisibly its weary line
Along the cloudless Main, he, in those hours
Of tiresome indolence, would often hang
Over the vessel's side, and gaze and gaze ;
And, while the broad blue wave and sparkling foam
Flashed round him images and hues that wrought
In union with the employment of his heart,
He, thus by feverish passion overcome,
Even with the organs of his bodily eye,
Below him, in the bosom of the deep,
Saw mountains ; saw the forms of sheep that grazed
On verdant hills—with dwellings among trees,
And shepherds clad in the same country grey
Which he himself had worn.
                                And now, at last,
From perils manifold, with some small wealth
Acquired by traffic 'mid the Indian Isles,
To his paternal home he is returned,
With a determined purpose to resume
The life he had lived there ; both for the sake
Of many darling pleasures, and the love
Which to an only brother he has borne
In all his hardships, since that happy time
When, whether it blew foul or fair, they two
Were brother shepherds on their native hills.
—They were the last of all their race : and now,
When Leonard had approached his home, his heart
Failed in him ; and, not venturing to inquire
Tidings of one so long and dearly loved,
He to the solitary churchyard turned ;

That, as he knew in what particular spot
His family were laid, he thence might learn
If still his Brother lived, or to the file
Another grave was added.   He had found
Another grave,—near which a full half-hour
He had remained : but, as he gazed, there grew
Such a confusion in his memory,
That he began to doubt ; and even to hope
That he had seen this heap of turf before,—
That it was not another grave ; but one
He had forgotten.   He had lost his path,
As up the vale, that afternoon, he walk'd
Through fields which once had been well known to him:
And oh ! what joy the recollection now
Sent to his heart ! he lifted up his eyes,
And looking round, imagined that he saw
Strange alteration wrought on every side
Among the woods and fields, and that the rocks,
And the eternal hills themselves were changed.

    By this the Priest, who down the field had come
Unseen by Leonard, at the churchyard gate
Stopp'd short,—and thence, at leisure, limb by limb,
Perused him with a gay complacency.
Ay, thought the Vicar, smiling to himself,
'Tis one of those who needs must leave the path
Of the world's business to go wild alone :
His arms have a perpetual holiday ;
The happy man will creep about the fields,
Following his fancies by the hour, to bring
Tears down his cheeks, or solitary smiles
Into his face, until the setting sun
Write fool upon his forehead.   Planted thus

Beneath a shed that over-arch'd the gate
Of this rude churchyard, till the stars appear'd,
The good Man might have communed with himself
But that the Stranger, who had left the grave,
Approach'd; he recognised the Priest at once,
And, after greetings interchanged, and given
By Leonard to the Vicar, as to one
Unknown to him, this dialogue ensued :—

LEONARD

You live, Sir, in these dales a quiet life :
Your years make up one peaceful family ;
And who would grieve and fret, if, welcome come
And welcome gone, they are so like each other,
They cannot be remember'd ?   Scarce a funeral
Comes to this churchyard once in eighteen months ;
And yet some changes must take place among you,
And you who dwell here, even among these rocks
Can trace the finger of mortality,
And see, that with her threescore years and ten,
We are not all that perish.——I remember,
For many years ago I pass'd this road,
There was a footway all along the fields
By the brook-side—'tis gone—and that dark cleft !
To me it does not seem to wear the face
Which then it had.

PRIEST

Nay, Sir, for aught I know
That chasm is much the same—

LEONARD

But, surely, yonder—

PRIEST

Ay, there, indeed, your memory is a friend
That does not play you false.—On that tall pike
(It is the loneliest place of all these hills)
There were two springs which bubbled side by
     side,
As if they had been made that they might be
Companions for each other : ten years back,
Close to those brother fountains, the huge crag
Was rent with lightning,—one is dead and gone,
The other, left behind, is flowing still.——
For accidents and changes such as these,
We want not store of them !—a waterspout
Will bring down half a mountain ; what a feast
For folks that wander up and down like you
To see an acre's breadth of that wide cliff
One roaring cataract :—a sharp May-storm,
Will come with loads of January snow,
And in one night send twenty score of sheep
To feed the ravens ; or a shepherd dies
By some untoward death among the rocks :
The ice breaks up and sweeps away a bridge—
A wood is fell'd :—and then for our own homes !
A child is born or christen'd, a field plough'd,
A daughter sent to service, a web spun,
The old house clock is deck'd with a new face ;
And hence, so far from wanting facts or dates
To chronicle the time, we all have here
A pair of diaries,—one serving, Sir,
For the whole dale, and one for each fireside—
Yours was a stranger's judgment : for historians,
Commend me to these valleys !

Leonard

                        Yet your Churchyard
Seems, if such freedom may be used with you,
To say that you are heedless of the past;
An orphan could not find his mother's grave:
Here's neither head nor foot stone, plate of brass,
Cross-bones or skull,—type of our earthly state
Or emblem of our hopes: the dead man's home
Is but a fellow to that pasture field.

Priest

Why, there, Sir, is a thought that's new to me!
The stone-cutters, 'tis true, might beg their bread
If every English churchyard were like ours;
Yet your conclusion wanders from the truth:
We have no need of names and epitaphs;
We talk about the dead by our firesides.
And then, for our immortal part; *we* want
No symbols, Sir, to tell us that plain tale:
The thought of death sits easy on the man
Who has been born and dies among the mountains.

Leonard

Your Dalesmen, then, do in each other's thoughts
Possess a kind of second life: no doubt
You, Sir, could help me to the history
Of half these graves?

Priest

                        For eight-score winters past,
With what I've witness'd, and with what I've heard,
Perhaps I might; and, on a winter's evening,

If you were seated at my chimney's nook,
By turning o'er these hillocks one by one,
We two could travel, Sir, through a strange round;
Yet all in the broad highway of the world.
Now there's a grave—your foot is half upon it,—
It looks just like the rest; and yet that man
Died broken-hearted.

LEONARD

                    'Tis a common case.
We'll take another: who is he that lies
Beneath yon ridge, the last of those three graves?
It touches on that piece of native rock
Left in the churchyard wall.

PRIEST

                    That's Walter Ewbank.
He had as white a head and fresh a cheek
As ever were produced by youth and age
Engendering in the blood of hale fourscore.
Through five long generations had the heart
Of Walter's forefathers o'erflow'd the bounds
Of their inheritance, that single cottage—
You see it yonder; and those few green fields.
They toil'd and wrought, and still from sire to son
Each struggled, and each yielded as before
A little—yet a little—and old Walter,
They left to him the family heart and land
With other burthens than the crop it bore.
Year after year the old man still kept up
A cheerful mind,—and buffeted with bond,
Interest, and mortgages; at last he sank,

And went into his grave before his time.
Poor Walter! whether it was care that spurr'd him,
God only knows, but to the very last
He had the lightest foot in Ennerdale:
His pace was never that of an old man:
I almost see him tripping down the path
With his two grandsons after him:—but you,
Unless our Landlord be your host to-night,
Have far to travel,—and on these rough paths
Even in the longest day of midsummer——

LEONARD

But those two Orphans——

PRIEST

Orphans!—Such they were—
Yet not while Walter lived:—for though their parents
Lay buried side by side, as now they lie,
The old man was a father to the boys,
Two fathers in one father: and if tears,
Shed when he talk'd of them where they were not,
And hauntings from the infirmity of love,
Are aught of what makes up a mother's heart,
This old Man, in the day of his old age,
Was half a mother to them.—If you weep, Sir,
To hear a stranger talking about strangers,
Heaven bless you when you are among your kindred!
Ay—you may turn that way—it is a grave
Which will bear looking at.

LEONARD

These boys—I hope
They loved this good old Man?—

PRIEST
                    They did—and truly:
But that was what we almost overlook'd.
They were such darlings of each other.   For
Though from their cradles they had lived with Walter,
The only kinsman near them, and though he
Inclined to them by reason of his age
With a more fond, familiar tenderness,
They, notwithstanding, had much love to spare,
And it all went into each other's hearts.
Leonard, the elder by just eighteen months,
Was two years taller: 'twas a joy to see,
To hear, to meet them!—From their house the school
Was distant three short miles—and in the time
Of storm and thaw, when every watercourse
And unbridged stream, such as you may have noticed
Crossing our roads at every hundred steps,
Was swoln into a noisy rivulet,
Would Leonard then, when elder boys perhaps
Remain'd at home, go staggering through the fords
Bearing his brother on his back.   I've seen him,
On windy days, in one of those stray brooks,
Ay, more than once I've seen him mid-leg deep,
Their two books lying both on a dry stone
Upon the hither side: and once I said,
As I remember, looking round these rocks
And hills on which we all of us were born,
That God who made the great book of the world
Would bless such piety—

LEONARD
                    It may be then—

PRIEST

Never did worthier lads break English bread ;
The very brightest Sunday Autumn saw,
With all its mealy clusters of ripe nuts,
Could never keep these boys away from church,
Or tempt them to an hour of Sabbath breach.
Leonard and James!   I warrant, every corner
Among these rocks, and every hollow place
Where foot could come, to one or both of them
Was known as well as to the flowers that grew there.
Like roebucks they went bounding o'er the hills :
They play'd like two young ravens on the crags :
Then they could write, ay, and speak too, as well
As many of their betters—and for Leonard!
The very night before he went away,
In my own house I put into his hand
A Bible, and I'd wager twenty pounds
That, if he is alive, he has it yet.

LEONARD

It seems these Brothers have not lived to be
A comfort to each other.—

PRIEST

                    That they might
Live to such end is what both old and young,
In this our valley, all of us, have wish'd,
And what, for my part, I have often pray'd :
But Leonard—

LEONARD

                    Then James still is left among you?

PRIEST

'Tis of the elder brother I am speaking:
They had an uncle;—he was at that time
A thriving man and traffick'd on the seas:
And, but for that same uncle, to this hour
Leonard had never handled rope or shroud.
For the boy loved the life which we lead here;
And, though of unripe years, a stripling only,
His soul was knit to this his native soil.
But, as I said, old Walter was too weak
To strive with such a torrent; when he died,
The estate and house were sold; and all their sheep,
A pretty flock, and which, for aught I know,
Had clothed the Ewbanks for a thousand years:—
Well—all was gone, and they were destitute;
And Leonard, chiefly for his Brother's sake,
Resolved to try his fortune on the seas.
'Tis now twelve years since we had tidings from him.
If there was one among us who had heard
That Leonard Ewbank was come home again,
From the Great Gavel, down by Leeza's banks,
And down the Enna, far as Egremont,
The day would be a very festival;
And those two bells of ours, which there you see—
Hanging in the open air—but, O good Sir!
This is sad talk—they'll never sound for him—
Living or dead.—When last we heard of him,
He was in slavery among the Moors
Upon the Barbary coast.—'Twas not a little
That would bring down his spirit; and no doubt,
Before it ended in his death, the Youth
Was sadly cross'd.—Poor Leonard! when we parted,

He took me by the hand and said to me,
If ever the day came when he was rich,
He would return, and on his father's land
He would grow old among us.

LEONARD

                If that day
Should come, 'twould needs be a glad day for him ;
He would himself, no doubt, be happy then
As any that should meet him—

PRIEST

                     Happy ! Sir—

LEONARD

You said his kindred all were in their graves,
And that he had one Brother—

PRIEST

                   That is but
A fellow-tale of sorrow.   From his youth
James, though not sickly, yet was delicate ;
And Leonard being always by his side,
Had done so many offices about him,
That, though he was not of a timid nature,
Yet still the spirit of a mountain boy
In him was somewhat check'd ; and when his
    Brother
Was gone to sea, and he was left alone,
The little colour that he had was soon
Stolen from his cheek ; he droop'd, and pined, and
    pined—

LEONARD

But these are all the graves of full-grown men!

PRIEST

Ay, Sir, that pass'd away : we took him to us ;
He was the child of all the dale—he lived
Three months with one, and six months with another ;
And wanted neither food, nor clothes, nor love :
And many, many happy days were his.
But, whether blithe or sad, 'tis my belief
His absent Brother still was at his heart.
And when he lived beneath our roof, we found
(A practice till this time unknown to him)
That often, rising from his bed at night,
He in his sleep would walk about, and sleeping
He sought his brother Leonard.—You are moved !
Forgive me, Sir—before I spoke to you,
I judged you most unkindly.

LEONARD

But this youth,
How did he die at last ?

PRIEST

One sweet May morning
(It will be twelve years since when Spring returns)
He had gone forth among the new-dropp'd lambs,
With two or three companions, whom it chanced
Some further business summon'd to a house
Which stands at the dale-head.   James, tired, perhaps,
Or from some other cause, remain'd behind.
You see yon precipice ; it almost looks

Like some vast building made of many crags;
And in the midst is one particular rock
That rises like a column from the vale,
Whence by our shepherds it is call'd THE PILLAR.
James pointed to its summit, over which
They all had purposed to return together,
And told them that he there would wait for them;
They parted, and his comrades pass'd that way
Some two hours after, but they did not find him
Upon the summit—at the appointed place.
Of this they took no heed; but one of them,
Going by chance, at night, into the house
Which at that time was James's home, there learn'd
That nobody had seen him all that day:
The morning came, and still he was unheard of:
The neighbours were alarm'd and to the brook
Some went, and some towards the lake: ere noon
They found him at the foot of that same rock—
Dead, and with mangled limbs.   The third day after
I buried him, poor Youth, and there he lies!

LEONARD

And that then *is* his grave?   Before his death
You said that he saw many happy years?

PRIEST

Ay, that he did—

LEONARD

        And all went well with him?—

PRIEST

If he had one, the youth had twenty homes.

LEONARD

And you believe, then, that his mind was easy?—

PRIEST

Yes, long before he died he found that time
Is a true friend to sorrow ; and unless
His thoughts were turn'd on Leonard's luckless
    fortune,
He talk'd about him with a cheerful love.

LEONARD

He could not come to an unhallow'd end !

PRIEST

Nay, God forbid !—You recollect I mention'd
A habit which disquietude and grief
Had brought upon him ; and we all conjectured
That, as the day was warm, he had lain down
Upon the grass, and, waiting for his comrades,
He there had fallen asleep ; that in his sleep
He to the margin of the precipice
Had walk'd, and from the summit had fallen headlong
And so no doubt he perish'd.   When the Youth
Fell, in his hand he must have grasp'd, we think,
His shepherd's staff ; for on that Pillar of rock
It had been caught mid-way ; and there for years
It hung—and moulder'd there.
              The Priest here ended.
The Stranger would have thank'd him, but he felt
A gushing from his heart that took away
The power of speech.   Both left the spot in silence ;

And Leonard, when they reach'd the churchyard gate,
As the Priest lifted up the latch, turn'd round,—
And, looking at the grave, he said, "My Brother!"
The Vicar did not hear the words: and now
He pointed towards his dwelling-place, entreating
That Leonard would partake his homely fare:
The other thank'd him with an earnest voice;
But added, that, the evening being calm,
He would pursue his journey. So they parted.

It was not long ere Leonard reach'd a grove
That overhung the road: he there stopp'd short.
And, sitting down beneath the trees, review'd
All that the Priest had said: his early years
Were with him in his heart—his cherish'd hopes,
And thoughts which had been his an hour before,
All press'd on him with such a weight, that now
This vale, where he had been so happy, seem'd
A place in which he could not bear to live:
So he relinquish'd all his purposes.
He travell'd back to Egremont: and thence,
That night, he wrote a letter to the Priest,
Reminding him of what had pass'd between them;
And adding, with a hope to be forgiven,
That it was from the weakness of his heart
He had not dared to tell him who he was.

This done, he went on shipboard, and is now
A Seaman, a grey-headed Mariner.

A FAREWELL

FAREWELL, thou little Nook of mountain
    ground,
Thou rocky corner in the lowest stair
Of that magnificent temple which doth bound
One side of our whole vale with grandeur rare;
Sweet garden-orchard, eminently fair,
The loveliest spot that man hath ever found,
Farewell!—we leave thee to Heaven's peaceful care,
Thee, and the Cottage which thou dost surround.

Our boat is safely anchor'd by the shore,
And there will safely ride when we are gone;
The flowering shrubs that deck our humble door
Will prosper, though untended and alone:
Fields, goods, and far-off chattels we have none:
These narrow bounds contain our private store
Of things earth makes and sun doth shine upon;
Here are they in our sight—we have no more.

Sunshine and shower be with you, bud and bell!
For two months now in vain we shall be sought;
We leave you here in solitude to dwell
With these our latest gifts of tender thought;
Thou, like the morning, in thy saffron coat
Bright gowan, and marsh-marigold, farewell!
Whom from the borders of the Lake we brought,
And placed together near our rocky Well.

We go for One to whom ye will be dear;
And she will prize this Bower, this Indian shed,
Our own contrivance, Building without peer!
A gentle Maid, whose heart is lowly bred,

Whose pleasures are in wild fields gatherèd,
With joyousness, and with a thoughtful cheer,
Will come to you,—to you herself will wed,—
And love the blessed life that we lead here.

Dear Spot! which we have watch'd with tender heed,
Bringing thee chosen plants and blossoms blown
Among the distant mountains, flower and weed,
Which thou hast taken to thee as thy own,
Making all kindness register'd and known;
Thou for our sakes, though Nature's child indeed,
Fair in thyself and beautiful alone,
Hast taken gifts which thou dost little need.

And O most constant, yet most fickle Place,
That hast thy wayward moods, as thou dost show
To them who look not daily on thy face;
Who, being loved, in love no bounds dost know,
And say'st, when we forsake thee, "Let them go!"
Thou easy-hearted Thing, with thy wild race
Of weeds and flowers, till we return be slow,
And travel with the year at a soft pace.

Help us to tell Her tales of years gone by,
And this sweet spring, the best beloved and best.
Joy will be flown in its mortality;
Something must stay to tell us of the rest.
Here, throng'd with primroses, the steep rock's
        breast
Glitter'd at evening like a starry sky;
And in this bush our sparrow built her nest,
Of which I sang one song that will not die.

O happy Garden! whose seclusion deep
Hath been so friendly to industrious hours;
And to soft slumbers, that did gently steep
Our spirits, carrying with them dreams of flowers,
And wild notes warbled among leafy bowers;
Two burning months let summer overleap,
And, coming back with Her who will be ours,
Into thy bosom we again shall creep.

   1802.

STANZAS

WRITTEN IN MY POCKET-COPY OF THOMSON'S 'CASTLE OF INDOLENCE'

WITHIN our happy Castle there dwelt One
    Whom without blame I may not overlook,
For never sun on living creature shone
Who more devout enjoyment with us took:
Here on his hours he hung as on a book,
On his own time here would he float away,
As doth a fly upon a summer brook;
But go to-morrow, or belike to-day,
Seek for him,—he is fled; and whither none can say.

Thus often would he leave our peaceful home,
And find elsewhere his business or delight;
Out of our Valley's limits did he roam:
Full many a time, upon a stormy night,
His voice came to us from the neighbouring height:
Oft could we see him driving full in view
At mid-day, when the sun was shining bright;
What ill was on him, what he had to do,
A mighty wonder bred among our quiet crew.

Ah! piteous sight it was to see this Man
When he came back to us, a withered flower,—
Or like a sinful creature, pale and wan.
Down would he sit; and without strength or power
Look at the common grass from hour to hour:
And oftentimes, how long I fear to say,
Where apple-trees in blossom made a bower,
Retired in that sunshiny shade he lay;
And, like a naked Indian, slept himself away.

Great wonder to our gentle tribe it was
Whenever from our Valley he withdrew;
For happier soul no living creature has
Than he had, being here the long day through.
Some thought he was a lover, and did woo:
Some thought far worse of him, and judged him
     wrong;
But verse was what he had been wedded to;
And his own mind did like a tempest strong
Come to him thus, and drove the weary Wight
     along.

With him there often walked in friendly guise,
Or lay upon the moss by brook or tree,
A noticeable Man with large grey eyes,
And a pale face that seemed undoubtedly
As if a blooming face it ought to be;
Heavy his low-hung lip did oft appear,
Deprest by weight of musing Phantasy;
Profound his forehead was, though not severe;
Yet some did think that he had little business
     here:

Sweet heaven forefend ! his was a lawful right ;
Noisy he was, and gamesome as a boy ;
His limbs would toss about him with delight,
Like branches when strong winds the trees annoy.
Nor lacked his calmer hours device or toy
To banish listlessness and irksome care ;
He would have taught you how you might employ
Yourself ; and many did to him repair,—
And certes not in vain ; he had inventions rare.

Expedients, too, of simplest sort he tried :
Long blades of grass, plucked round him as he lay,
Made, to his ear attentively applied,
A pipe on which the wind would deftly play ;
Glasses he had, that little things display,
The beetle panoplied in gems and gold,
A mailèd angel on a battle-day ;
The mysteries that cups of flowers enfold,
And all the gorgeous sights which fairies do behold.

He would entice that other Man to hear
His music, and to view his imagery ;
And, sooth, these two were each to the other dear :
No livelier love in such a place could be :
There did they dwell—from earthly labour free,
As happy spirits as were ever seen ;
If but a bird, to keep them company,
Or butterfly sate down, they were, I ween,
As pleased as if the same had been a Maiden
    queen.

  1802.

LUCY

STRANGE fits of passion have I known:
  And I will dare to tell,
But in the Lover's ear alone,
  What once to me befell.

When she I loved looked every day
  Fresh as a rose in June,
I to her cottage bent my way,
  Beneath an evening moon.

Upon the moon I fixed my eye,
  All over the wide lea;
With quickening pace my horse drew nigh
  Those paths so dear to me.

And now we reached the orchard-plot;
  And, as we climbed the hill,
The sinking moon to Lucy's cot
  Came near, and nearer still.

In one of those sweet dreams I slept,
  Kind Nature's gentlest boon!
And all the while my eyes I kept
  On the descending moon.

My horse moved on; hoof after hoof
  He raised, and never stopped:
When down behind the cottage-roof,
  At once, the bright moon dropped.

What fond and wayward thoughts will slide
Into a Lover's head!
'O mercy!' to myself I cried,
'If Lucy should be dead!'

   1799.

LUCY DEAD

SHE dwelt among the untrodden ways
   Beside the springs of Dove,
A Maid whom there were none to praise,
   And very few to love :

A violet by a mossy stone
   Half hidden from the eye!
Fair as a star, when only one
   Is shining in the sky.

She lived unknown, and few could know
   When Lucy ceased to be ;
But she is in her grave, and, oh,
   The difference to me!

   1790.

THE AFFLICTION OF MARGARET ——

WHERE art thou, my beloved Son,
   Where art thou, worse to me than dead?
Oh find me, prosperous or undone!
Or, if the grave be now thy bed,
Why am I ignorant of the same,
That I may rest ; and neither blame
Nor sorrow may attend thy name?

D

Seven years, alas! to have received
No tidings of an only child;
To have despaired, have hoped, believed,
And been for evermore beguiled;
Sometimes with thoughts of very bliss!
I catch at them, and then I miss;
Was ever darkness like to this?

He was among the prime in worth,
An object beauteous to behold;
Well born, well bred; I sent him forth
Ingenuous, innocent, and bold:
If things ensued that wanted grace,
As hath been said, they were not base;
And never blush was on my face.

Ah! little doth the young-one dream,
When full of play and childish cares,
What power is in his wildest scream,
Heard by his mother unawares!
He knows it not, he cannot guess:
Years to a mother bring distress;
But do not make her love the less.

Neglect me! no, I suffered long
From that ill thought; and, being blind,
Said, 'Pride shall help me in my wrong,
Kind mother have I been, as kind
As ever breathed:' and that is true;
I've wet my path with tears like dew,
Weeping for him when no one knew.

My Son, if thou be humbled, poor,
Hopeless of honour and of gain,
Oh ! do not dread thy mother's door ;
Think not of me with grief and pain :
I now can see with better eyes ;
And worldly grandeur I despise,
And fortune with her gifts and lies.

Alas ! the fowls of heaven have wings,
And blasts of heaven will aid their flight ;
They mount—how short a voyage brings
The wanderers back to their delight !
Chains tie us down by land and sea ;
And wishes, vain as mine, may be
All that is left to comfort thee.

Perhaps some dungeon hears thee groan,
Maimed, mangled by inhuman men ;
Or thou upon a desert thrown
Inheritest the lion's den ;
Or hast been summoned to the deep,
Thou, thou and all thy mates, to keep
An incommunicable sleep.

I look for ghosts ; but none will force
Their way to me : 'tis falsely said
That there was ever intercourse
Between the living and the dead ;
For, surely, then I should have sight
Of him I wait for day and night,
With love and longings infinite.

My apprehensions come in crowds;
I dread the rustling of the grass;
The very shadows of the clouds
Have power to shake me as they pass:
I question things and do not find
One that will answer to my mind;
And all the world appears unkind.

Beyond participation lie
My troubles, and beyond relief:
If any chance to heave a sigh,
They pity me, and not my grief.
Then come to me, my Son, or send
Some tidings that my woes may end;
I have no other earthly friend!
   1804.

THE CHILDLESS FATHER

'UP, Timothy, up with your staff and away!
    Not a soul in the village this morning will
   stay;
The hare has just started from Hamilton's
   grounds,
And Skiddaw is glad with the cry of the hounds.'

—Of coats and of jackets grey, scarlet, and green,
On the slopes of the pastures all colours were seen;
With their comely blue aprons, and caps white as
   snow,
The girls on the hills made a holiday show.

Fresh sprigs of green boxwood, not six months
   before,
Filled the funeral basin [1] at Timothy's door;
A coffin through Timothy's threshold had pass'd;
One Child did it bear, and that Child was his last.

Now fast up the dell came the noise and the fray,
The horse and the horn, and the 'Hark! hark away!'
Old Timothy took up his staff, and he shut
With a leisurely motion the door of his hut.

Perhaps to himself at that moment he said,
'The key I must take, for my Ellen is dead.'
But of this in my ears not a word did he speak;
And he went to the chase with a tear on his cheek.

   1800.

MICHAEL

A PASTORAL POEM

IF from the public way you turn your steps
   Up the tumultuous brook of Greenhead Ghyll,
You will suppose that with an upright path
Your feet must struggle; in such bold ascent
The pastoral mountains front you, face to face.
But, courage! for around that boisterous brook
The mountains have all opened out themselves,

---

[1] In several parts of the North of England, when a funeral takes
place, a basin full of sprigs of boxwood is placed at the door of
the house from which the coffin is taken up, and each person who
attends the funeral ordinarily takes a sprig of this boxwood, and
throws it into the grave of the deceased.

And made a hidden valley of their own.
No habitation can be seen ; but they
Who journey thither find themselves alone
With a few sheep, with rocks and stones, and
      kites
That overhead are sailing in the sky.
It is in truth an utter solitude ;
Nor should I have made mention of this Dell
But for one object which you might pass by,
Might see and notice not.   Beside the brook
Appears a straggling heap of unhewn stones :
And to that simple object appertains
A story—unenriched with strange events,
Yet not unfit, I deem, for the fireside,
Or for the summer shade.   It was the first
Of those domestic tales that spake to me
Of Shepherds, dwellers in the valleys, men
Whom I already loved ;—not verily
For their own sakes, but for the fields and hills
Where was their occupation and abode.
And hence this Tale, while I was yet a Boy
Careless of books, yet having felt the power
Of Nature, by the gentle agency
Of natural objects, led me on to feel
For passions that were not my own, and think
(At random and imperfectly indeed)
On man, the heart of man, and human life.
Therefore, although it be a history
Homely and rude, I will relate the same
For the delight of a few natural hearts ;
And, with yet fonder feeling, for the sake
Of youthful Poets, who among these hills
Will be my second self when I am gone.

Upon the forest-side in Grasmere Vale
There dwelt a Shepherd, Michael was his name;
An old man, stout of heart, and strong of limb.
His bodily frame had been from youth to age
Of an unusual strength: his mind was keen,
Intense, and frugal, apt for all affairs,
And in his shepherd's calling he was prompt
And watchful more than ordinary men.
Hence had he learned the meaning of all winds,
Of blasts of every tone: and, oftentimes,
When others heeded not, he heard the South
Make subterraneous music, like the noise
Of bagpipers on distant Highland hills.
The Shepherd, at such warning, of his flock
Bethought him, and he to himself would say,
'The winds are now devising work for me!'
And, truly, at all times, the storm, that drives
The traveller to a shelter, summoned him
Up to the mountains: he had been alone
Amid the heart of many thousand mists,
That came to him, and left him, on the heights.
So lived he till his eightieth year was past.
And grossly that man errs, who should suppose
That the green valleys, and the streams and
      rocks,
Were things indifferent to the Shepherd's thoughts.
Fields, where with cheerful spirits he had breathed
The common air; hills, which with vigorous step
He had so often climbed; which had impressed
So many incidents upon his mind
Of hardship, skill or courage, joy or fear;
Which, like a book, preserved the memory
Of the dumb animals whom he had saved,

Had fed or sheltered, linking to such acts
The certainty of honourable gain ;
Those fields, those hills—what could they less?—
    had laid
Strong hold on his affections, were to him
A pleasurable feeling of blind love,
The pleasure which there is in life itself.

    His days had not been passed in singleness.
His Helpmate was a comely matron, old—
Though younger than himself full twenty years.
She was a woman of a stirring life,
Whose heart was in her house : two wheels she had
Of antique form ; this large, for spinning wool ;
That small, for flax ; and if one wheel had rest
It was because the other was at work.
The Pair had but one inmate in their house,
An only Child, who had been born to them
When Michael, telling o'er his years, began
To deem that he was old,—in shepherd's phrase,
With one foot in the grave.   This only Son,
With two brave sheep-dogs tried in many a storm,
The one of an inestimable worth,
Made all their household.   I may truly say
That they were as a proverb in the vale
For endless industry.   When day was gone,
And from their occupations out of doors
The Son and Father were come home, even then
Their labour did not cease ; unless when all
Turned to the cleanly supper-board, and there,
Each with a mess of pottage and skimmed milk,
Sat round the basket piled with oaten cakes,

And their plain home-made cheese. Yet when the
    meal
Was ended, Luke (for so the Son was named)
And his old Father both betook themselves
To such convenient work as might employ
Their hands by the fireside; perhaps to card
Wool for the Housewife's spindle, or repair
Some injury done to sickle, flail, or scythe,
Or other implement of house or field.

   Down from the ceiling, by the chimney's edge,
That in our ancient uncouth country style
With huge and black projection overbrowed
Large space beneath, as duly as the light
Of day grew dim the Housewife hung a lamp;
An aged utensil, which had performed
Service beyond all others of its kind.
Early at evening did it burn—and late,
Surviving comrade of uncounted hours,
Which, going by from year to year, had found,
And left the couple neither gay perhaps
Nor cheerful, yet with objects and with hopes,
Living a life of eager industry.
And now, when Luke had reached his eighteenth year,
There by the light of this old lamp they sate,
Father and Son, while far into the night
The Housewife plied her own peculiar work,
Making the cottage through the silent hours
Murmur as with the sound of summer flies.
This light was famous in its neighbourhood,
And was a public symbol of the life
That thrifty Pair had lived.   For, as it chanced,
Their cottage on a plot of rising ground

Stood single, with large prospect, north and south,
High into Easedale, up to Dunmail-Raise,
And westward to the village near the lake ;
And from this constant light, so regular
And so far seen, the House itself, by all
Who dwelt within the limits of the vale,
Both old and young, was named THE EVENING STAR.

Thus living on through such a length of years,
The Shepherd, if he loved himself, must needs
Have loved his Helpmate ; but to Michael's heart
This son of his old age was yet more dear—
Less from instinctive tenderness, the same
Fond spirit that blindly works in the blood of all—
Than that a child, more than all other gifts
That earth can offer to declining man,
Brings hope with it, and forward-looking thoughts,
And stirrings of inquietude, when they
By tendency of nature needs must fail.
Exceeding was the love he bare to him,
His heart and his heart's joy ! For oftentimes
Old Michael, while he was a babe in arms,
Had done him female service, not alone
For pastime and delight, as is the use
Of fathers, but with patient mind enforced
To acts of tenderness ; and he had rocked
His cradle, as with a woman's gentle hand.

And, in a later time, ere yet the Boy
Had put on boy's attire, did Michael love,
Albeit of a stern unbending mind,
To have the Young-one in his sight, when he
Wrought in the field. or on his shepherd's stool

Sate with a fettered sheep before him stretched
Under the large old oak, that near his door
Stood single, and, from matchless depth of shade,
Chosen for the Shearer's covert from the sun,
Thence in our rustic dialect was called
THE CLIPPING TREE,[1] a name which yet it bears.
There, while they two were sitting in the shade,
With others round them, earnest all and blithe,
Would Michael exercise his heart with looks
Of fond correction and reproof bestowed
Upon the Child, if he disturbed the sheep
By catching at their legs, or with his shouts
Scared them, while they lay still beneath the shears.

And when by Heaven's good grace the boy grew up
A healthy Lad, and carried in his cheek
Two steady roses that were five years old ;
Then Michael from a winter coppice cut
With his own hand a sapling, which he hooped
With iron, making it throughout in all
Due requisites a perfect shepherd's staff,
And gave it to the Boy ; wherewith equipt
He as a watchman oftentimes was placed
At gate or gap, to stem or turn the flock ;
And, to his office prematurely called,
There stood the urchin, as you will divine,
Something between a hindrance and a help ;
And for this cause not always, I believe,
Receiving from his Father hire of praise ;
Though nought was left undone which staff, or voice,
Or looks, or threatening gestures, could perform.

[1] Clipping is the word used in the North of England for shearing.

But soon as Luke, full ten years old, could stand
Against the mountain blasts, and to the heights,
Not fearing toil, nor length of weary ways,
He with his Father daily went, and they
Were as companions, why should I relate
That objects which the Shepherd loved before
Were dearer now? that from the Boy there came
Feelings and emanations—things which were
Light to the sun and music to the wind;
And that the old Man's heart seemed born again?

Thus in his Father's sight the Boy grew up:
And now, when he had reached his eighteenth year,
He was his comfort and his daily hope.

While in this sort the simple household lived
From day to day, to Michael's ear there came
Distressful tidings.   Long before the time
Of which I speak, the Shepherd had been bound
In surety for his brother's son, a man
Of an industrious life, and ample means;
But unforeseen misfortunes suddenly
Had prest upon him; and old Michael now
Was summoned to discharge the forfeiture,
A grievous penalty, but little less
Than half his substance.   This unlooked-for claim,
At the first hearing, for a moment took
More hope out of his life than he supposed
That any old man ever could have lost.
As soon as he had armed himself with strength
To look his trouble in the face, it seemed
The Shepherd's sole resource to sell at once
A portion of his patrimonial fields.

Such was his first resolve; he thought again,
And his heart failed him. 'Isabel,' said he,
Two evenings after he had heard the news,
'I have been toiling more than seventy years,
And in the open sunshine of God's love
Have we all lived; yet if these fields of ours
Should pass into a stranger's hand, I think
That I could not lie quiet in my grave.
Our lot is a hard lot; the sun himself
Has scarcely been more diligent than I;
And I have lived to be a fool at last
To my own family. An evil man
That was, and made an evil choice, if he
Were false to us; and if he were not false,
There are ten thousand to whom loss like this
Had been no sorrow. I forgive him;—but
'Twere better to be dumb than to talk thus.

'When I began, my purpose was to speak
Of remedies and of a cheerful hope.
Our Luke shall leave us, Isabel; the land
Shall not go from us, and it shall be free;
He shall possess it, free as is the wind
That passes over it. We have, thou know'st,
Another kinsman—he will be our friend
In this distress. He is a prosperous man,
Thriving in trade—and Luke to him shall go,
And with this kinsman's help and his own thrift
He quickly will repair this loss, and then
He may return to us. If here he stay,
What can be done? Where every one is poor
What can be gained?'
                              At this the old Man paused,

And Isabel sat silent, for her mind
Was busy looking back into past times.
There's Richard Bateman, thought she to herself,
He was a parish-boy—at the church-door
They made a gathering for him, shillings, pence
And halfpennies, wherewith the neighbours bought
A basket, which they filled with pedlar's wares;
And, with this basket on his arm, the lad
Went up to London, found a master there,
Who, out of many, chose the trusty boy
To go and overlook his merchandise
Beyond the seas , where he grew wondrous rich,
And left estates and monies to the poor,
And, at his birthplace, built a chapel floored
With marble, which he sent from foreign lands.
These thoughts, and many others of like sort,
Passed quickly through the mind of Isabel,
And her face brightened.   The old Man was glad,
And thus resumed : 'Well, Isabel ! this scheme
These two days has been meat and drink to me.
Far more than we have lost is left us yet.
—We have enough—I wish indeed that I
Were younger ;—but this hope is a good hope.
—Make ready Luke's best garments, of the best
Buy for him more, and let us send him forth
To-morrow, or the next day, or to-night :
—If he *could* go, the Boy should go to-night.'

Here Michael ceased, and to the fields went forth
With a light heart.   The Housewife for five days
Was restless morn and night, and all day long
Wrought on with her best fingers to prepare
Things needful for the journey of her son.

But Isabel was glad when Sunday came
To stop her in her work : for, when she lay
By Michael's side, she through the last two nights
Heard him, how he was troubled in his sleep :
And when they rose at morning she could see
That all his hopes were gone.   That day at noon
She said to Luke, while they two by themselves
Were sitting at the door, ' Thou must not go :
We have no other Child but thee to lose,
None to remember—do not go away,
For if thou leave thy Father he will die.'
The Youth made answer with a jocund voice ;
And Isabel, when she had told her fears,
Recovered heart.   That evening her best fare
Did she bring forth, and all together sat
Like happy people round a Christmas fire.

With daylight Isabel resumed her work ;
And all the ensuing week the house appeared
As cheerful as a grove in Spring : at length
The expected letter from their kinsman came,
With kind assurances that he would do
His utmost for the welfare of the Boy ;
To which requests were added that forthwith
He might be sent to him.   Ten times or more
The letter was read over ; Isabel
Went forth to show it to the neighbours round ;
Nor was there at that time on English land
A prouder heart than Luke's.   When Isabel
Had to her house returned, the old Man said,
' He shall depart to-morrow.'   To this word
The Housewife answered, talking much of things
Which, if at such short notice he should go,

Would surely be forgotten.   But at length
She gave consent, and Michael was at ease.

   Near the tumultuous brook of Greenhead Ghyll,
In that deep valley, Michael had designed
To build a Sheepfold ; and, before he heard
The tidings of his melancholy loss,
For this same purpose he had gathered up
A heap of stones, which by the streamlet's edge
Lay thrown together, ready for the work.
With Luke that evening thitherward he walked :
And soon as they had reached the place he stopped,
And thus the old Man spake to him : ' My Son,
To-morrow thou wilt leave me : with full heart
I look upon thee, for thou art the same
That wert a promise to me ere thy birth,
And all thy life hast been my daily joy.
I will relate to thee some little part
Of our two histories ; 'twill do thee good
When thou art from me, even if I should touch
On things thou canst not know of.——After thou
First cam'st into the world—as oft befalls
To new-born infants—thou didst sleep away
Two days, and blessings from thy Father's tongue
Then fell upon thee.   Day by day passed on,
And still I loved thee with increasing love.
Never to living ear came sweeter sounds
Than when I heard thee by our own fireside
First uttering, without words, a natural tune ;
While thou, a feeding babe, didst in thy joy
Sing at thy Mother's breast.   Month followed month,
And in the open fields my life was passed
And on the mountains : else I think that thou

Hadst been brought up upon thy Father's knees.
But we were playmates, Luke: among these hills,
As well thou knowest, in us the old and young
Have played together, nor with me didst thou
Lack any pleasure which a boy can know.'
Luke had a manly heart; but at these words
He sobbed aloud. The old Man grasped his hand,
And said, 'Nay, do not take it so—I see
That these are things of which I need not speak.
—Even to the utmost I have been to thee
A kind and a good Father: and herein
I but repay a gift which I myself
Received at others' hands; for, though now old
Beyond the common life of man, I still
Remember them who loved me in my youth.
Both of them sleep together: here they lived,
As all their Forefathers had done; and when
At length their time was come, they were not loth
To give their bodies to the family mould.
I wished that thou shouldst live the life they lived:
But, 'tis a long time to look back, my Son,
And see so little gain from threescore years,
These fields were burthened when they came to me;
Till I was forty years of age, not more
Than half of my inheritance was mine.
I toiled and toiled; God blessed me in my work,
And till these three weeks past the land was free.
—It looks as if it never could endure
Another Master. Heaven forgive me, Luke,
If I judge ill for thee, but it seems good
That thou shouldst go.'

              At this the old Man paused;
Then, pointing to the stones near which they stood,

Thus, after a short silence, he resumed:
'This was a work for us; and now, my Son,
It is a work for me. But, lay one stone—
Here, lay it for me, Luke, with thine own hands.
Nay, Boy, be of good hope;—we both may live
To see a better day. At eighty-four
I still am strong and hale; do thou thy part;
I will do mine.—I will begin again
With many tasks that were resigned to thee:
Up to the heights, and in among the storms,
Will I without thee go again, and do
All works which I was wont to do alone,
Before I knew thy face.—Heaven bless thee,
    Boy!
Thy heart these two weeks has been beating fast
With many hopes; it should be so—yes—yes—
I knew that thou couldst never have a wish
To leave me, Luke: thou hast been bound to me
Only by links of love: when thou art gone,
What will be left to us!—But, I forget
My purposes. Lay now the corner-stone,
As I requested; and hereafter, Luke,
When thou art gone away, should evil men
Be thy companions, think of me, my Son,
And of this moment: hither turn thy thoughts,
And God will strengthen thee: amid all fear
And all temptation, Luke, I pray that thou
May'st bear in mind the life thy Fathers lived,
Who, being innocent, did for that cause
Bestir them in good deeds. Now, fare thee well—
When thou return'st, thou in this place wilt see
A work which is not here: a covenant
'Twill be between us; but, whatever fate

Befall thee, I shall love thee to the last,
And bear thy memory with me to the grave.'

  The Shepherd ended here; and Luke stooped
    down
And, as his Father had requested, laid
The first stone of the Sheepfold.   At the sight
The old Man's grief broke from him; to his heart
He pressed his Son, he kissèd him and wept;
And to the house together they returned.
—Hushed was that House in peace, or seeming
    peace,
Ere the night fell :—with morrow's dawn the Boy
Began his journey, and when he had reached
The public way, he put on a bold face;
And all the neighbours, as he passed their doors,
Came forth with wishes and with farewell prayers,
That followed him till he was out of sight.

  A good report did from their Kinsman come,
Of Luke and his well-doing : and the Boy
Wrote loving letters, full of wondrous news,
Which, as the Housewife phrased it, were throughout
'The prettiest letters that were ever seen.'
Both parents read them with rejoicing hearts.
So, many months passed on : and once again
The Shepherd went about his daily work
With confident and cheerful thoughts; and now
Sometimes when he could find a leisure hour
He to that valley took his way, and there
Wrought at the Sheepfold.   Meantime Luke began
To slacken in his duty; and at length,
He in the dissolute city gave himself

To evil courses : ignominy and shame
Fell on him, so that he was driven at last
To seek a hiding-place beyond the seas.

There is a comfort in the strength of love;
'Twill make a thing endurable, which else
Would overset the brain, or break the heart :
I have conversed with more than one who well
Remember the old Man, and what he was
Years after he had heard this heavy news.
His bodily frame had been from youth to age
Of an unusual strength.   Among the rocks
He went, and still looked up to sun and cloud,
And listened to the wind : and, as before,
Performed all kinds of labour for his sheep,
And for the land, his small inheritance.
And to that hollow dell from time to time
Did he repair, to build the Fold of which
His flock had need.   'Tis not forgotten yet
The pity which was then in every heart
For the old Man—and 'tis believed by all
That many and many a day he thither went,
And never lifted up a single stone.

There, by the Sheepfold, sometimes was he seen
Sitting alone, or with his faithful Dog,
Then old, beside him lying at his feet.
The length of full seven years, from time to time,
He at the building of this Sheepfold wrought,
And left the work unfinished when he died.
Three years, or little more, did Isabel
Survive her Husband : at her death the estate
Was sold, and went into a stranger's hand.

The Cottage which was named THE EVENING STAR
Is gone—the ploughshare has been through the
    ground
On which it stood: great changes have been
    wrought
In all the neighbourhood:—yet the oak is left
That grew beside their door; and the remains
Of the unfinished Sheepfold may be seen
Beside the boisterous brook of Greenhead Ghyll.

    1800.

POEMS ON THE NAMING OF PLACES

TO JOANNA

AMID the smoke of cities did you pass
    The time of early youth; and there you
    learned,
From years of quiet industry, to love
The living Beings by your own fireside,
With such a strong devotion that your heart
Is slow to meet the sympathies of them
Who look upon the hills with tenderness,
And make dear friendships with the streams and
    groves.
Yet we, who are transgressors in this kind,
Dwelling retired in our simplicity
Among the woods and fields, we love you well,
Joanna! and I guess, since you have been
So distant from us now for two long years,
That you will gladly listen to discourse,
However trivial, if you thence be taught
That they, with whom you once were happy,
    talk
Familiarly of you and of old times.

While I was seated, now some ten days past,
Beneath those lofty firs, that overtop
Their ancient neighbour, the old steeple-tower,
The Vicar from his gloomy house hard by
Came forth to greet me; and when he had
    asked,
'How fares Joanna, that wild-hearted Maid!
And when will she return to us?' he paused;
And, after short exchange of village news,
He with grave looks demanded, for what cause,
Reviving obsolete idolatry,
I, like a Runic Priest, in characters
Of formidable size had chiselled out
Some uncouth name upon the native rock,
Above the Rotha, by the forest-side.
—Now, by those dear immunities of heart
Engendered between malice and true love,
I was not loth to be so catechised,
And this was my reply: 'As it befell,
One summer morning we had walked abroad
At break of day, Joanna and myself.
—'Twas that delightful season when the broom,
Full-flowered, and visible in every steep,
Along the copses runs in veins of gold.
Our pathway led us on to Rotha's banks;
And when we came in front of that tall rock
That eastward looks, I there stopped short—
    and stood
Tracing the lofty barrier with my eye
From base to summit; such delight I found
To note in shrub and tree, in stone and flower,
That intermixture of delicious hues,
Along so vast a surface, all at once,

In one impression, by connecting force
Of their own beauty, imaged in the heart.
—When I had gazed perhaps two minutes' space,
Joanna, looking in my eyes, beheld
That ravishment of mine, and laughed aloud.
The Rock, like something starting from a sleep,
Took up the Lady's voice, and laughed again;
That ancient Woman seated on Helm Crag
Was ready with her cavern; Hammar Scar,
And the tall Steep of Silver How, sent forth
A noise of laughter; southern Loughrigg heard,
And Fairfield answered with a mountain tone;
Helvellyn far into the clear blue sky
Carried the Lady's voice,—old Skiddaw blew
His speaking-trumpet;—back out of the clouds
Of Glaramara southward came the voice;
And Kirkstone tossed it from his misty head.
—Now whether (said I to our cordial Friend,
Who in the heyday of astonishment
Smiled in my face) this were in simple truth
A work accomplished by the brotherhood
Of ancient mountains, or my ear was touched
With dreams and visionary impulses
To me alone imparted, sure I am
That there was a loud uproar in the hills.
And, while we both were listening, to my side
The fair Joanna drew, as if she wished
To shelter from some object of her fear.
—And hence, long afterwards, when eighteen
     moons
Were wasted, as I chanced to walk alone
Beneath this rock, at sunrise, on a calm
And silent morning, I sat down, and there,

In memory of affections old and true,
I chiselled out in those rude characters
Joanna's name deep in the living stone:—
And I, and all who dwell by my fireside,
Have called the lovely rock, JOANNA'S ROCK.'
1800.

Note.—In Cumberland and Westmoreland are several Inscriptions upon the native rock, which, from the wasting of time, and the rudeness of the workmanship, have been mistaken for Runic. They are without doubt Roman.

The Rotha, mentioned in this poem, is the River which, flowing through the lakes of Grasmere and Rydale, falls into Wynander-mere. On Helm Crag, that impressive single mountain at the head of the Vale of Grasmere, is a rock which from most points of view bears a striking resemblance to an old Woman cowering. Close by this rock is one of these fissures or caverns which in the language of the country are called dungeons. Most of the mountains here mentioned immediately surround the Vale of Grasmere; of the others, some are at a considerable distance, but they belong to the same cluster.

WORDSWORTH'S PEAK

THERE is an Eminence,—of these our hills
    The last that parleys with the setting sun;
We can behold it from our orchard-seat;
And, when at evening we pursue our walk
Along the public way, this Peak, so high
Above us, and so distant in its height,
Is visible: and often seems to send
Its own deep quiet to restore our hearts.
The meteors make of it a favourite haunt:
The star of Jove, so beautiful and large
In the mid heavens, is never half so fair
As when he shines above it.   'Tis in truth'

The loneliest place we have among the clouds.
And She who dwells with me, whom I have
      loved
With such communion that no place on earth
Can ever be a solitude to me,
Hath to this lonely Summit given my Name.
    1800.

POINT RASH-JUDGMENT

A NARROW girdle of rough stones and crags,
      A rude and natural causeway, interposed
Between the water and a winding slope
Of copse and thicket, leaves the eastern shore
Of Grasmere safe in its own privacy :
And there myself and two beloved Friends,
One calm September morning, ere the mist
Had altogether yielded to the sun,
Sauntered on this retired and difficult way,
——Ill suits the road with one in haste ; but we
Played with our time ; and, as we strolled along,
It was our occupation to observe
Such objects as the waves had tossed ashore—
Feather, or leaf, or weed, or withered bough,
Each on the other heaped, along the line
Of the dry wreck.   And, in our vacant mood,
Not seldom did we stop to watch some tuft
Of dandelion seed or thistle's beard,
That skimmed the surface of the dead calm lake,
Suddenly halting now—a lifeless stand !
And starting off again with freak as sudden ;
In all its sportive wanderings, all the while,

Making report of an invisible breeze,
That was its wings, its chariot, and its horse,
Its playmate, rather say, its moving soul.
——And often, trifling with a privilege
Alike indulged to all, we paused, one now,
And now the other, to point out, perchance,
To pluck, some flower or water-weed, too fair
Either to be divided from the place
On which it grew, or to be left alone
To its own beauty.   Many such there are,
Fair ferns and flowers, and chiefly that tall fern,
So stately, of the queen Osmunda named ;
Plant lovelier, in its own retired abode
On Grasmere's beach, than Naiad by the side
Of Grecian brook, or Lady of the Mere,
Sole-sitting by the shores of old romance.
—So fared we that bright morning : from the fields,
Meanwhile, a noise was heard, the busy mirth
Of reapers, men and women, boys and girls.
Delighted much to listen to those sounds,
And feeding thus our fancies, we advanced
Along the indented shore ; when suddenly,
Through a thin veil of glittering haze was seen
Before us, on a point of jutting land,
The tall and upright figure of a Man
Attired in peasant's garb, who stood alone,
Angling beside the margin of the lake.
'Improvident and reckless,' we exclaimed,
'The Man must be, who thus can lose a day
Of the mid harvest, when the labourer's hire
Is ample, and some little might be stored
Wherewith to cheer him in the winter time.'
Thus talking of that Peasant, we approached

Close to the spot where with his rod and line
He stood alone; whereat he turned his head
To greet us—and we saw a Man worn down
By sickness, gaunt and lean, with sunken cheeks
And wasted limbs, his legs so long and lean
That for my single self I looked at them,
Forgetful of the body they sustained.—
Too weak to labour in the harvest field,
The Man was using his best skill to gain
A pittance from the dead unfeeling lake
That knew not of his wants.   I will not say
What thoughts immediately were ours, nor how
The happy idleness of that sweet morn,
With all its lovely images, was changed
To serious musing and to self-reproach.
Nor did we fail to see within ourselves
What need there is to be reserved in speech,
And temper all our thoughts with charity.
—Therefore, unwilling to forget that day,
My Friend, Myself, and She who then received
The same admonishment, have called the place
By a memorial name, uncouth indeed
As e'er by mariner was given to bay
Or foreland, on a new-discovered coast;
And POINT RASH-JUDGMENT is the name it bears.

   1800.

POEMS OF THE FANCY

A MORNING EXERCISE

FANCY, who leads the pastimes of the glad,
    Full oft is pleased a wayward dart to throw;
Sending sad shadows after things not sad,
Peopling the harmless fields with signs of woe:
Beneath her sway, a simple forest cry
Becomes an echo of man's misery.

Blithe ravens croak of death; and when the owl
Tries his two voices for a favourite strain—
Tu-whit—tu-whoo! the unsuspecting fowl
Forebodes mishap or seems but to complain;
Fancy, intent to harass and annoy,
Can thus pervert the evidence of joy.

Through border wilds where naked Indians stray,
Myriads of notes attest her subtle skill;
A feathered taskmaster cries, 'WORK AWAY!'
And, in thy iteration, 'WHIP POOR WILL!'[1]
Is heard the spirit of a toil-worn slave,
Lashed out of life, not quiet in the grave.

[1] See Waterton's 'Wanderings in South America.'

What wonder? at her bidding, ancient lays
Steeped in dire grief the voice of Philomel;
And that fleet messenger of summer days,
The Swallow, twittered subject to like spell;
But ne'er could Fancy bend the buoyant Lark
To melancholy service—hark! O hark!

The daisy sleeps upon the dewy lawn,
Not lifting yet the head that evening bowed;
But *He* is risen, a later star of dawn,
Glittering and twinkling near yon rosy cloud;
Bright gem instinct with music, vocal spark;
The happiest bird that sprang out of the Ark!

Hail, blest above all kinds!—Supremely skilled
Restless with fixed to balance, high with low,
Thou leav'st the halcyon free her hopes to build,
On such forbearance as the deep may show;
Perpetual flight, unchecked by earthly ties,
Leav'st to the wandering bird of paradise.

Faithful, though swift as lightning, the meek dove;
Yet more hath Nature reconciled in thee;
So constant with thy downward eye of love,
Yet, in aerial singleness, so free;
So humble, yet so ready to rejoice
In power of wing and never-wearied voice.

To the last point of vision, and beyond,
Mount, daring warbler!—that love-prompted strain
('Twixt thee and thine a never-failing bond)
Thrills not the less the bosom of the plain:
Yet might'st thou seem, proud privilege! to sing
All independent of the leafy spring.

How would it please old Ocean to partake,
With sailors longing for a breeze in vain,
The harmony thy notes most gladly make
Where earth resembles most his own domain!
Urania's self might welcome with pleased ear
These matins mounting towards her native sphere.

Chanter by heaven attracted, whom no bars
To daylight known deter from that pursuit,
'Tis well that some sage instinct, when the stars
Come forth at evening, keeps Thee still and mute;
For not an eyelid could to sleep incline
Wert thou among them, singing as they shine!

1828.

TO THE DAISY

' Her[1] divine skill taught me this,
That from everything I saw
I could some instruction draw,
And raise pleasure to the height
Through the meanest object's sight.
By the murmur of a spring,
Or the least bough's rustelling;
By a Daisy whose leaves spread
Shut when Titan goes to bed;
Or a shady bush or tree;
She could more infuse in me
Than all Nature's beauties can
In some other wiser man.'

G. WITHER.

IN youth from rock to rock I went,
    From hill to hill, in discontent
Of pleasure high and turbulent,
    Most pleased when most uneasy;

---

[1] His muse.

But now my own delights I make,—
My thirst at every rill can slake,
And gladly Nature's love partake,
    Of Thee, sweet Daisy!

Thee Winter in the garland wears
That thinly decks his few grey hairs,
Spring parts the clouds with softest airs,
    That she may sun thee;
Whole Summer fields are thine by right;
And Autumn, melancholy Wight!
Doth in thy crimson head delight
    When rains are on thee.

In shoals and bands, a morrice train,
Thou greet'st the traveller in the lane;
Pleased at his greeting thee again;
    Yet nothing daunted,
Nor grieved if thou be set at nought:
And oft alone in nooks remote
We meet thee, like a pleasant thought,
    When such are wanted.

Be violets in their secret mews
The flowers the wanton Zephyrs choose;
Proud be the rose, with rains and dews
    Her head impearling;
Thou liv'st with less ambitious aim,
Yet hast not gone without thy fame;
Thou art indeed, by many a claim,
    The Poet's darling.

If to a rock from rains he fly,
Or, some bright day of April sky,
Imprisoned by hot sunshine lie
    Near the green holly,
And wearily at length should fare;
He needs but look about, and there
Thou art!—a friend at hand, to scare
    His melancholy.

A hundred times, by rock or bower,
Ere thus I have lain couched an hour,
Have I derived from thy sweet power
    Some apprehension;
Some steady love; some brief delight;
Some memory that had taken flight;
Some chime of fancy, wrong or right,
    Or stray invention.

If stately passions in me burn,
And one chance look to Thee should turn,
I drink out of an humbler urn
    A lowlier pleasure;
The homely sympathy that heeds
The common life our nature breeds;
A wisdom fitted to the needs
    Of hearts at leisure.

Fresh smitten by the morning ray,
When thou art up, alert and gay,
Then, cheerful Flower! my spirits play
    With kindred gladness:

And when at dusk by dews opprest
Thou sink'st, the image of thy rest
Hath often eased my pensive breast
    Of careful sadness.

And all day long I number yet,
All seasons through, another debt,
Which I, wherever thou art met,
    To thee am owing ;
An instinct call it, a blind sense ;
A happy, genial influence,
Coming one knows not how, nor whence,
    Nor whither going.

Child of the Year ! that round dost run
Thy pleasant course,—when day's begun
As ready to salute the sun
    As lark or leveret,
Thy long-lost praise thou shalt regain ;
Nor be less dear to future men
Than in old time ;—thou not in vain
    Art Nature's favourite.[1]

1802.

TO THE SAME FLOWER

WITH little here to do and see
    Of things that in the great world be,
Daisy ! again I talk to thee,
    For thou art worthy :

[1] See, in Chaucer and the elder poets, the honours formerly paid to this flower.

Thou unassuming Common-place
Of Nature, with that homely face,
And yet with something of a grace
    Which Love makes for thee !

Oft on the dappled turf at ease
I sit, and play with similes,
Loose types of things through all degrees,
    Thoughts of thy raising :
And many a fond and idle name
I give to thee, for praise or blame,
As is the humour of the game,
    While I was gazing.

A nun demure of lowly port ;
Or sprightly maiden, of Love's court,
In thy simplicity the sport
    Of all temptations ;
A queen in crown of rubies drest ;
A starveling in a scanty vest ;
Are all, as seems to suit thee best,
    Thy appellations.

A little Cyclops, with one eye
Staring to threaten and defy,
That thought comes next—and instantly
    The freak is over.
The shape will vanish, and behold !
A silver shield with boss of gold,
That spreads itself, some faery bold
    In fight to cover.

I see thee glittering from afar—
And then thou art a pretty star;
Not quite so fair as many are
　　In heaven above thee!
Yet like a star, with glittering crest,
Self-poised in air thou seem'st to rest;—
May peace come never to his nest
　　Who shall reprove thee!

Bright *Flower!* for by that name at last,
When all my reveries are past,
I call thee, and to that cleave fast,
　　Sweet silent creature!
That breath'st with me in sun and air,
Do thou, as thou art wont, repair
My heart with gladness, and a share
　　Of thy meek nature!
　　1805.

THE GREEN LINNET

BENEATH these fruit-tree boughs that shed
　　Their snow-white blossoms on my head
With brightest sunshine round me spread
　　Of spring's unclouded weather,
In this sequestered nook how sweet
To sit upon my orchard-seat!
And birds and flowers once more to greet,
　　My last year's friends together.

One have I marked, the happiest guest
In all this covert of the blest:
Hail to Thee, far above the rest
　　In joy of voice and pinion!

Thou, Linnet! in thy green array,
Presiding Spirit here to-day,
Dost lead the revels of the May;
    And this is thy dominion.

While birds, and butterflies, and flowers,
Make all one band of paramours,
Thou, ranging up and down the bowers,
    Art sole in thy employment;
A Life, a Presence like the Air,
Scattering thy gladness without care,
Too blest with any one to pair;
    Thyself thy own enjoyment.

Amid yon tuft of hazel trees,
That twinkle to the gusty breeze,
Behold him perched in ecstasies,
    Yet seeming still to hover;
There! where the flutter of his wings
Upon his back and body flings
Shadows and sunny glimmerings,
    That cover him all over.

My dazzled sight he oft deceives,
A Brother of the dancing leaves;
Then flits, and from the cottage eaves
    Pours forth his song in gushes;
As if by that exulting strain
He mocked and treated with disdain
The voiceless Form he chose to feign,
    While fluttering in the bushes.

1803.

TO A SKY-LARK

UP with me! up with me into the clouds!
　　For thy song, Lark, is strong;
Up with me, up with me into the clouds!
　　　Singing, singing,
With clouds and sky about thee ringing,
　　Lift me, guide me till I find
That spot which seems so to thy mind!

I have walked through wildernesses dreary,
　　And to-day my heart is weary;
　　Had I now the wings of a Faery,
　　　Up to thee would I fly.
There is madness about thee, and joy divine
　　　In that song of thine;
Lift me, guide me, high and high
To thy banqueting-place in the sky!

　　　Joyous as morning,
Thou art laughing and scorning;
Thou hast a nest for thy love and thy rest,
And, though little troubled with sloth,
Drunken Lark! thou wouldst be loth
To be such a traveller as I.
　　Happy, happy Liver!
With a soul as strong as a mountain river,
Pouring out praise to the almighty Giver,
　　Joy and jollity be with us both!

Alas! my journey, rugged and uneven,
Through prickly moors or dusty ways must wind;

But hearing thee, or others of thy kind,
As full of gladness and as free of heaven,
I, with my fate contented, will plod on,
And hope for higher raptures, when life's day is
    done.

  1805.

TO THE SMALL CELANDINE[1]

PANSIES, lilies, kingcups, daisies,
    Let them live upon their praises;
Long as there's a sun that sets,
Primroses will have their glory;
Long as there are violets,
They will have a place in story:
There's a flower that shall be mine,
'Tis the little Celandine.

Eyes for some men travel far
For the finding of a star;
Up and down the heavens they go,
Men that keep a mighty rout!
I'm as great as they, I trow,
Since the day I found thee out,
Little Flower!—I'll make a stir,
Like a sage astronomer.

Modest, yet withal an Elf
Bold, and lavish of thyself;

---

[1] Common Pilewort.

Since we needs must first have met
I have seen thee, high and low,
Thirty years or more, and yet
'Twas a face I did not know;
Thou hast now, go where I may,
Fifty greetings in a day.

Ere a leaf is on a bush,
In the time before the thrush
Has a thought about her nest,
Thou wilt come with half a call,
Spreading out thy glossy breast
Like a careless Prodigal;
Telling tales about the sun,
When we've little warmth, or none.

Poets, vain men in their mood!
Travel with the multitude;
Never heed them; I aver
That they all are wanton wooers.
But the thrifty cottager,
Who stirs little out of doors,
Joys to spy thee near her home:
Spring is coming—Thou art come!

Comfort have thou of thy merit,
Kindly, unassuming Spirit!
Careless of thy neighbourhood,
Thou dost show thy pleasant face
On the moor, and in the wood,
In the lane—there's not a place,
Howsoever mean it be,
But 'tis good enough for thee.

Ill befall the yellow flowers,
Children of the flaring hours !
Buttercups, that will be seen,
Whether we will see or no ;
Others, too, of lofty mien ;
They have done as worldlings do,
Taken praise that should be thine,
Little, humble Celandine !

Prophet of delight and mirth,
Ill-requited upon earth ;
Herald of a mighty band,
Of a joyous train ensuing,
Serving at my heart's command,
Tasks that are no tasks renewing,
I will sing, as doth behove,
Hymns in praise of what I love !

   1803.

TO THE SAME FLOWER

PLEASURES newly found are sweet
    When they lie about our feet :
February last, my heart
First at sight of thee was glad ;
All unheard of as thou art,
Thou must needs, I think, have had,
Celandine ! and long ago,
Praise of which I nothing know.

I have not a doubt but he,
Whosoe'er the man might be,

Who the first with pointed rays
(Workman worthy to be sainted)
Set the sign-board in a blaze,
When the rising sun he painted,
Took the fancy from a glance
At thy glittering countenance.

Soon as gentle breezes bring
News of winter's vanishing,
And the children build their bowers,
Sticking 'kerchief-plots of mould
All about with full-blown flowers,
Thick as sheep in shepherd's fold!
With the proudest thou art there,
Mantling in the tiny square.

Often have I sighed to measure
By myself a lonely pleasure,
Sighed to think, I read a book,
Only read, perhaps, by me;
Yet I long could overlook
Thy bright coronet and Thee,
And thy arch and wily ways,
And thy store of other praise.

Blithe of heart, from week to week
Thou dost play at hide-and-seek;
While the patient primrose sits
Like a beggar in the cold,
Thou, a flower of wiser wits,
Slipp'st into thy sheltering hold;

Liveliest of the vernal train
When ye are all out again.

Drawn by what peculiar spell,
By what charm of sight or smell,
Does the dim-eyed curious bee,
Labouring for her waxen cells,
Fondly settle upon Thee,
Prized above all buds and bells
Opening daily at thy side,
By the season multiplied?

Thou art not beyond the moon,
 But a thing 'beneath our shoon;'
Let the bold Discoverer thrid
In his bark the polar sea;
Rear who will a pyramid;
Praise it is enough for me,
If there be but three or four
Who will love my little Flower.
    1803.

STRAY PLEASURES

'——*Pleasure is spread through the earth*
In stray gifts, to be claimed by whoever shall find.'

BY their floating mill,
     That lies dead and still,
Behold yon Prisoners three!
The Miller with two Dames, on the breast of the
    Thames!
The platform is small, but gives room for them all;
And they're dancing merrily.

From the shore come the notes
　　To their mill where it floats,
To their house and their mill tethered fast;
To the small wooden isle where, their work to beguile,
They from morning to even take whatever is given;—
And many a blithe day they have past.

In sight of the spires,
　　All alive with the fires
Of the sun going down to his rest,
In the broad open eye of the solitary sky,
They dance,—there are three, as jocund as free,
While they dance on the calm river's breast.

Man and Maidens wheel,
　　They themselves make the reel,
And their music's a prey which they seize;
It plays not for them,—what matter! 'tis theirs;
And if they had care, it has scattered their cares,
While they dance, crying, 'Long as ye please!'

They dance not for me,
　　Yet mine is their glee!
Thus pleasure is spread through the earth
In stray gifts, to be claimed by whoever shall find;
Thus a rich loving-kindness, redundantly kind,
Moves all nature to gladness and mirth.

The showers of the spring
　　Rouse the birds, and they sing;
If the wind do but stir for his proper delight,
Each leaf, that and this, his neighbour will kiss;
Each wave, one and t'other, speeds after his brother;
They are happy, for that is their right!

1806.

POEMS OF THE IMAGINATION

THERE WAS A BOY

THERE was a Boy; ye knew him well, ye cliffs
    And islands of Winander! Many a time,
At evening, when the earliest stars began
To move along the edges of the hills,
Rising or setting, would he stand alone,
Beneath the trees, or by the glimmering lake;
And there, with fingers interwoven, both hands
Pressed closely palm to palm and to his mouth
Uplifted, he, as through an instrument,
Blew mimic hootings to the silent owls,
That they might answer him. And they would
    shout
Across the watery vale, and shout again,
Responsive to his call,—with quivering peals
And long halloos, and screams, and echoes loud
Redoubled and redoubled; concourse wild
Of jocund din! And, when there came a pause
Of silence such as baffled his best skill:
Then, sometimes, in that silence, while he hung
Listening, a gentle shock of mild surprise
Has carried far into his heart the voice
Of mountain torrents; or the visible scene
Would enter unawares into his mind

With all its solemn imagery, its rocks,
Its woods, and that uncertain heaven received
Into the bosom of the steady lake.

   This boy was taken from his mates, and died
In childhood, ere he was full twelve years old.
Pre-eminent in beauty is the vale
Where he was born and bred : the churchyard hangs
Upon a slope above the village school ;
And, through that churchyard when my way has led
On summer evenings, I believe, that there
A long half-hour together I have stood
Mute—looking at the grave in which he lies !
   1799.

TO THE CUCKOO

O BLITHE New-comer ! I have heard,
     I hear thee and rejoice :
O Cuckoo ! shall I call thee Bird,
Or but a wandering Voice ?

While I am lying on the grass
Thy twofold shout I hear,
From hill to hill it seems to pass,
At once far off and near !

Though babbling only to the Vale,
Of sunshine and of flowers ;
Thou bringest unto me a tale
Of visionary hours.

Thrice welcome, darling of the Spring!
Even yet thou art to me
No bird, but an invisible thing
A voice, a mystery;

The same whom in my schoolboy days
I listened to; that Cry
Which made me look a thousand ways
In bush, and tree, and sky.

To seek thee did I often rove
Through woods and on the green;
And thou wert still a hope, a love;
Still longed for, never seen!

And I can listen to thee yet!
Can lie upon the plain
And listen, till I do beget
That golden time again.

O blessed Bird! the earth we pace
Again appears to be
An unsubstantial, fairy place;
That is fit home for Thee!

   1804.

A NIGHT-PIECE

THE sky is overcast
    With a continuous cloud of texture close,
Heavy and wan, all whitened by the Moon,
Which through that veil is indistinctly seen,
A dull contracted circle, yielding light
So feebly spread, that not a shadow falls,

Chequering the ground, from rock, plant, tree, or tower.
At length a pleasant instantaneous gleam
Startles the pensive traveller while he treads
His lonesome path, with unobserving eye
Bent earthwards ; he looks up—the clouds are split
Asunder,—and above his head he sees
The clear Moon, and the glory of the heavens.
There, in a black-blue vault she sails along,
Followed by multitudes of stars, that, small
And sharp, and bright, along the dark abyss
Drive as she drives.   How fast they wheel away,
Yet vanish not !—the wind is in the tree,
But they are silent ;—still they roll along
Immeasurably distant ; and the vault,
Built round by those white clouds, enormous clouds,
Still deepens its unfathomable depth.
At length the Vision closes ; and the mind,
Not undisturbed by the delight it feels,
Which slowly settles into peaceful calm,
Is left to muse upon the solemn scene.

1798.

YEW-TREES

THERE is a Yew-tree, pride of Lorton Vale,
    Which to this day stands single, in the midst
Of its own darkness, as it stood of yore,
Not loth to furnish weapons for the bands
Of Umfraville or Percy, ere they marched
To Scotland's heaths ; or those that crossed the sea
And drew their sounding bows at Azincour,
Perhaps at earlier Crecy, or Poictiers.
Of vast circumference and gloom profound

This solitary Tree! a living thing
Produced too slowly ever to decay;
Of form and aspect too magnificent
To be destroyed.   But worthier still of note
Are those fraternal Four of Borrowdale,
Joined in one solemn and capacious grove;
Huge trunks!—and each particular trunk a growth
Of intertwisted fibres serpentine
Up-coiling, and inveterately convolved,—
Nor uninformed with Phantasy, and looks
That threaten the profane;—a pillared shade,
Upon whose grassless floor of red-brown hue,
By sheddings from the pining umbrage tinged
Perennially—beneath whose sable roof
Of boughs, as if for festal purpose, decked
With unrejoicing berries—ghostly Shapes
May meet at noontide; Fear and trembling Hope,
Silence and Foresight; Death the Skeleton
And Time the Shadow;—there to celebrate,
As in a natural temple scattered o'er
With altars undisturbed of mossy stone,
United worship; or in mute repose
To lie and listen to the mountain flood
Murmuring from Glaramara's inmost caves.

1803.

NUTTING

IT seems a day
    (I speak of one from many singled out),
One of those heavenly days that cannot die;
When, in the eagerness of boyish hope,
I left our cottage threshold, sallying forth

With a huge wallet o'er my shoulders slung,
A nutting-crook in hand; and turned my steps
Tow'rd some far-distant wood, a Figure quaint,
Tricked out in proud disguise of cast-off weeds
Which for that service had been husbanded,
By exhortation of my frugal Dame—
Motley accoutrement, of power to smile
At thorns, and brakes, and brambles,—and, in truth,
More raggèd than need was! O'er pathless rocks,
Through beds of matted fern and tangled thickets,
Forcing my way, I came to one dear nook
Unvisited, where not a broken bough
Drooped with its withered leaves, ungracious sign
Of devastation; but the hazels rose
Tall and erect, with tempting clusters hung,
A virgin scene!—A little while I stood,
Breathing with such suppression of the heart
As joy delights in; and, with wise restraint
Voluptuous, fearless of a rival, eyed
The banquet;—or beneath the trees I sate
Among the flowers, and with the flowers I played;
A temper known to those who, after long
And weary expectation, have been blest
With sudden happiness beyond all hope.
Perhaps it was a bower beneath whose leaves
The violets of five seasons reappear
And fade, unseen by any human eye;
Where fairy water-breaks do murmur on
For ever; and I saw the sparkling foam,
And with my cheek on one of those green stones
That, fleeced with moss, under the shady trees,
Lay round me, scattered like a flock of sheep,
I heard the murmur and the murmuring sound,

In that sweet mood when pleasure loves to pay
Tribute to ease; and, of its joy secure,
The heart luxuriates with indifferent things,
Wasting its kindliness on stocks and stones,
And on the vacant air.   Then up I rose,
And dragged to earth both branch and bough, with
    crash
And merciless ravage: and the shady nook
Of hazels, and the green and mossy bower,
Deformed and sullied, patiently gave up
Their quiet being: and, unless I now
Confound my present feelings with the past,
Ere from the mutilated bower I turned
Exulting, rich beyond the wealth of kings,
I felt a sense of pain when I beheld
The silent trees, and saw the intruding sky.
Then, dearest Maiden, move along these shades
In gentleness of heart; with gentle hand
Touch—for there is a spirit in the woods.

  1799.

THE SIMPLON PASS

BROOK and road
    Were fellow-travellers in this gloomy Pass,
And with them did we journey several hours
At a slow step.   The immeasurable height
Of woods decaying, never to be decayed,
The stationary blasts of waterfalls
And in the narrow rent, at every turn,
Winds thwarting winds bewildered and forlorn,
The torrents shooting from the clear blue sky,
The rocks that muttered close upon our ears,

Black drizzling crags that spake by the wayside
As if a voice were in them, the sick sight
And giddy prospect of the raving stream,
The unfettered clouds and region of the heavens,
Tumult and peace, the darkness and the light—
Were all like workings of one mind, the features
Of the same face, blossoms upon one tree,
Characters of the great Apocalypse,
The types and symbols of Eternity,
Of first, and last, and midst, and without end.

1799.

A PERFECT WOMAN

SHE was a Phantom of delight
    When first she gleamed upon my sight;
A lovely Apparition, sent
To be a moment's ornament;
Her eyes as stars of Twilight fair,
Like Twilight's, too, her dusky hair;
But all things else about her drawn
From May-time and the cheerful Dawn;
A dancing Shape, an Image gay,
To haunt, to startle, and waylay.

I saw her upon nearer view,
A Spirit, yet a Woman too!
Her household motions light and free,
And steps of virgin liberty;
A countenance in which did meet
Sweet records, promises as sweet;
A Creature not too bright or good
For human nature's daily food;

For transient sorrows, simple wiles,
Praise, blame, love, kisses, tears, and smiles.

And now I see with eye serene
The very pulse of the machine;
A Being breathing thoughtful breath,
A traveller between life and death;
The reason firm, the temperate will,
Endurance, foresight, strength, and skill;
A perfect Woman, nobly planned,
To warn, to comfort, and command;
And yet a Spirit still, and bright
With something of angelic light.

   1804.

THE NIGHTINGALE

O NIGHTINGALE! thou surely art
    A creature of a ' fiery heart : '—
These notes of thine—they pierce and pierce;
Tumultuous harmony and fierce!
Thou sing'st as if the God of wine
Had helped thee to a Valentine;
A song in mockery and despite
Of shades, and dews, and silent night;
And steady bliss, and all the loves
Now sleeping in these peaceful groves.

I heard a Stock-dove sing or say
His homely tale, this very day;
His voice was buried among trees,
Yet to be come at by the breeze:

He did not cease ; but cooed—and cooed ;
And somewhat pensively he wooed :
He sang of love, with quiet blending,
Slow to begin, and never ending ;
Of serious faith, and inward glee ;
That was the song—the song for me !
   1806.

LUCY'S MEMORY

THREE years she grew in sun and shower,
   Then Nature said, ' A lovelier flower
On earth was never sown :
This Child I to myself will take :
She shall be mine, and I will make
A Lady of my own.

' Myself will to my darling be
Both law and impulse ; and with me
The Girl, in rock and plain,
In earth and heaven, in glade and bower
Shall feel an overseeing power
To kindle or restrain.

' She shall be sportive as the fawn
That wild with glee across the lawn
Or up the mountain springs ;
And hers shall be the breathing balm,
And hers the silence and the calm
Of mute insensate things.

' The floating clouds their state shall lend
To her ; for her the willow bend ;

Nor shall she fail to see
Even in the motions of the Storm
Grace that shall mould the Maiden's form
By silent sympathy.

'The stars of midnight shall be dear
To her; and she shall lean her ear
In many a secret place
Where rivulets dance their wayward round,
And beauty born of murmuring sound
Shall pass into her face.

'And vital feelings of delight
Shall rear her form to stately height,
Her virgin bosom swell ;
Such thoughts to Lucy I will give
While she and I together live
Here in this happy dell.'

Thus Nature spake.   The work was done—
How soon my Lucy's race was run !
She died, and left to me
This heath, this calm, and quiet scene ;
The memory of what has been,
And never more will be.

   1799.

THE LOVE FOR THE DEAD

A SLUMBER did my spirit seal ;
    I had no human fears :
She seemed a thing that could not feel
    The touch of earthly years.

No motion has she now, no force;
   She neither hears nor sees;
Rolled round in earth's diurnal course,
   With rocks, and stones, and trees.

   1799.

THE INWARD EYE

I WANDERED lonely as a cloud
      That floats on high o'er vales and hills,
When all at once I saw a crowd,
A host, of golden daffodils;
Beside the lake, beneath the trees,
Fluttering and dancing in the breeze.

Continuous as the stars that shine
And twinkle on the Milky Way,
They stretched in never-ending line
Along the margin of a bay:
Ten thousand saw I at a glance,
Tossing their heads in sprightly dance.

The waves beside them danced; but they
Outdid the sparkling waves in glee:
A poet could not but be gay,
In such a jocund company:
I gazed—and gazed—but little thought
What wealth the show to me had brought:

For oft, when on my couch I lie
In vacant or in pensive mood,
They flash upon that inward eye
Which is the bliss of solitude;
And then my heart with pleasure fills,
And dances with the daffodils.

   1804.

THE REVERIE OF POOR SUSAN

AT the corner of Wood Street, when daylight
    appears,
Hangs a Thrush that sings loud—it has sung for three
    years :
Poor Susan has passed by the spot, and has heard
In the silence of morning the song of the bird.

'Tis a note of enchantment ; what ails her ? She sees
A mountain ascending, a vision of trees ;
Bright volumes of vapour through Lothbury glide,
And a river flows on through the vale of Cheapside.

Green pastures she views in the midst of the dale,
Down which she so often has tripped with her pail ;
And a single small cottage, a nest like a dove's,
The one only dwelling on earth that she loves.

She looks, and her heart is in heaven : but they fade,
The mist and the river, the hill and the shade :
The stream will not flow, and the hill will not rise,
And the colours have all passed away from her eyes !
  1797.

POWER OF MUSIC

AN Orpheus ! an Orpheus ! yes, faith may grow
    bold,
And take to herself all the wonders of old ;—
Near the stately Pantheon you'll meet with the same
In the street that from Oxford hath borrowed its name.

His station is there ; and he works on the crowd,
He sways them with harmony merry and loud ;
He fills with his power all their hearts to the brim—
Was aught ever heard like his fiddle and him?

What an eager assembly ! what an empire is this !
The weary have life, and the hungry have bliss ;
The mourner is cheered, and the anxious have rest ;
And the guilt-burthened soul is no longer opprest.

As the Moon brightens round her the clouds of the
    night,
So He, where he stands, is a centre of light ;
It gleams on the face, there, of dusky-browed Jack,
And the pale-visaged Baker's, with basket on back.

That errand-bound 'Prentice was passing in haste—
What matter ! he's caught—and his time runs to
    waste ;
The Newsman is stopped, though he stops on the fret ;
And the half-breathless Lamplighter—he's in the net !

The Porter sits down on the weight which he bore ;
The Lass with her barrow wheels hither her store ;—
If a thief could be here he might pilfer at ease ;
She sees the Musician, 'tis all that she sees !

He stands, backed by the wall ;—he abates not his
    din ;
His hat gives him vigour, with boons dropping in,
From the old and the young, from the poorest ; and
    there !
The one-pennied Boy has his penny to spare.

O blest are the hearers, and proud be the hand
Of the pleasure it spreads through so thankful a band;
I am glad for him, blind as he is!—all the while
If they speak 'tis to praise, and they praise with a smile.

That tall Man, a giant in bulk and in height,
Not an inch of his body is free from delight;
Can he keep himself still, if he would? oh, not he!
The music stirs in him like wind through a tree.

Mark that Cripple who leans on his crutch; like a
    tower
That long has leaned forward, leans hour after hour!—
That Mother, whose spirit in fetters is bound,
While she dandles the Babe in her arms to the sound.

Now, coaches and chariots! roar on like a stream;
Here are twenty souls happy as souls in a dream:
They are deaf to your murmurs—they care not for
    you,
Nor what ye are flying, nor what ye pursue!
    1806.

STAR-GAZERS

WHAT crowd is this—what have we here? we
    must not pass it by;
A Telescope upon its frame, and pointed to the sky:
Long is it as a barber's pole, or mast of little boat,
Some little pleasure-skiff, that doth on Thames's
    waters float.

The Showman chooses well his place, 'tis Leicester's
  busy square;
And is as happy in his night, for the heavens are blue
  and fair;
Calm, though impatient, is the crowd; each stands
  ready with the fee,
And envies him that's looking;—what an insight must
  it be!

Yet, Showman, where can lie the cause? Shall thy
  Implement have blame,
A boaster, that when he is tried, fails, and is put to
  shame?
Or is it good as others are, and be their eyes in fault?
Their eyes, or minds? or, finally, is yon resplendent
  vault?

Is nothing of that radiant pomp so good as we have
  here?
Or gives a thing but small delight that never can be
  dear?
The silver moon with all her vales, and hills of
  mightiest fame,
Doth she betray us when they're seen? or are they but
  a name?

Or is it rather that Conceit rapacious is and strong,
And bounty never yields so much but it seems to do
  her wrong?
Or is it, that when human Souls a journey long have
  had
And are returned into themselves, they cannot but be
  sad?

Or must we be constrained to think that these Spec-
tators rude,
Poor in estate, of manners base, men of the multitude,
Have souls which never yet have risen, and therefore
prostrate lie?
No, no, this cannot be;—men thirst for power and
majesty!

Does, then, a deep and earnest thought the blissful
mind employ
Of him who gazes, or has gazed? a grave and steady joy,
That doth reject all show of pride, admits no outward
sign,
Because not of this noisy world, but silent and divine!

Whatever be the cause, 'tis sure that they who pry and
pore
Seem to meet with little gain, seem less happy than
before:
One after One they take their turn, nor have I one
espied
That doth not slackly go away, as if dissatisfied.

1806.

WRITTEN IN MARCH

WHILE RESTING ON THE BRIDGE AT THE FOOT
OF BROTHER'S WATER

THE Cock is crowing,
    The stream is flowing,
The small birds twitter,
The lake doth glitter,
The green field sleeps in the sun;

The oldest and youngest
Are at work with the strongest;
The cattle are grazing,
Their heads never raising;
There are forty feeding like one!

Like an army defeated
The snow hath retreated,
And now doth fare ill
On the top of the bare hill;
The Ploughboy is whooping—anon—anon:
    There's joy in the mountains;
    There's life in the fountains;
    Small clouds are sailing,
    Blue sky prevailing;
The rain is over and gone!

    1801.

BEGGARS

WHERE are they now, those wanton Boys?
    For whose free range the dædal earth
Was filled with animated toys,
And implements of frolic mirth;
With tools for ready wit to guide;
And ornaments of seemlier pride,
More fresh, more bright, than princes wear;
For what one moment flung aside
Another could repair;
What good or evil have they seen
Since I their pastime witnessed here,
Their daring wiles, their sportive cheer?
I ask—but all is dark between!

They met me in a genial hour,
When universal nature breathed
As with the breath of one sweet flower,—
A time to overrule the power
Of discontent, and check the birth
Of thoughts with better thoughts at strife,
The most familiar bane of life
Since parting Innocence bequeathed
Mortality to Earth!
Soft clouds, the whitest of the year,
Sailed through the sky—the brooks ran clear;
The lambs from rock to rock were bounding;
With songs the budded groves resounding;
And to my heart are still endeared
The thoughts with which it then was cheered;
The faith which saw that gladsome pair
Walk through the fire with unsinged hair.
Or, if such faith must needs deceive—
Then, Spirits of beauty and of grace,
Associates in that eager chase;
Ye, who within the blameless mind
Your favourite seat of empire find—
Kind Spirits! may we not believe
That they, so happy and so fair
Through your sweet influence, and the care
Of pitying Heaven, at least were free
From touch of *deadly* injury?
Destined, whate'er their earthly doom,
For mercy and immortal bloom!

1817.

RUTH

WHEN Ruth was left half-desolate,
    Her Father took another Mate;
And Ruth, not seven years old,
A slighted child, at her own will
Went wandering over dale and hill,
In thoughtless freedom, bold.

And she had made a pipe of straw,
And music from that pipe could draw
Like sounds of winds and floods;
Had built a bower upon the green,
As if she from her birth had been
An infant of the woods.

Beneath her father's roof, alone
She seemed to live; her thoughts her own;
Herself her own delight;
Pleased with herself, nor sad, nor gay;
And, passing thus the live-long day,
She grew to woman's height.

There came a Youth from Georgia's shore—
A military casque he wore,
With splendid feathers drest;
He brought them from the Cherokees;
The feathers nodded in the breeze,
And made a gallant crest.

From Indian blood you deem him sprung:
But no! he spake the English tongue,

And bore a soldier's name;
And, when America was free
From battle and from jeopardy,
He 'cross the ocean came.

With hues of genius on his cheek
In finest tones the Youth could speak:
—While he was yet a boy,
The moon, the glory of the sun,
And streams that murmur as they run,
Had been his dearest joy.

He was a lovely Youth! I guess
The panther in the wilderness
Was not so fair as he;
And, when he chose to sport and play,
No dolphin ever was so gay
Upon the tropic sea.

Among the Indians he had fought,
And with him many tales he brought
Of pleasure and of fear;
Such tales as told to any maid
By such a Youth, in the green shade,
Were perilous to hear.

He told of girls—a happy rout!
Who quit their fold with dance and shout,
Their pleasant Indian town,
To gather strawberries all day long;
Returning with a choral song
When daylight is gone down.

He spake of plants that hourly change
Their blossoms, through a boundless range
Of intermingling hues;
With budding, fading, faded flowers
They stand the wonder of the bowers
From morn to evening dews.

He told of the magnolia, spread
High as a cloud, high over head!
The cypress and her spire;
—Of flowers that with one scarlet gleam
Cover a hundred leagues, and seem
To set the hills on fire.

The Youth of green savannahs spake,
And many an endless, endless lake,
With all its fairy crowds
Of islands, that together lie
As quietly as spots of sky
Among the evening clouds.

'How pleasant,' then he said, 'it were
A fisher or a hunter there,
In sunshine or in shade
To wander with an easy mind;
And build a household fire, and find
A home in every glade!

'What days and what bright years! Ah me!
Our life were life indeed, with thee
So passed in quiet bliss,
And all the while,' said he, 'to know
That we were in a world of woe,
On such an earth as this!'

And then he sometimes interwove
Fond thoughts about a father's love:
'For there,' said he, 'are spun
Around the heart such tender ties,
That our own children to our eyes
Are dearer than the sun.

'Sweet Ruth! and could you go with me
My helpmate in the woods to be,
Our shed at night to rear;
Or run, my own adopted bride,
A sylvan huntress at my side,
And drive the flying deer!

'Beloved Ruth!'—no more he said.
The wakeful Ruth at midnight shed
A solitary tear:
She thought again—and did agree
With him to sail across the sea,
And drive the flying deer.

'And now, as fitting is and right,
We in the church our faith will plight,
A husband and a wife.'
Even so they did; and I may say
That to sweet Ruth that happy day
Was more than human life.

Through dream and vision did she sink,
Delighted all the while to think
That on those lonesome floods,
And green savannahs, she should share
His board with lawful joy, and bear
His name in the wild woods.

But, as you have before been told,
This Stripling, sportive, gay, and bold,
And, with his dancing crest,
So beautiful, through savage lands
Had roamed about, with vagrant bands
Of Indians in the West.

The wind, the tempest roaring high,
The tumult of a tropic sky,
Might well be dangerous food
For him, a Youth to whom was given
So much of earth—so much of heaven,
And such impetuous blood.

Whatever in those climes he found
Irregular in sight or sound
Did to his mind impart
A kindred impulse, seemed allied
To his own powers, and justified
The workings of his heart.

Nor less, to feed voluptuous thought,
The beauteous forms of nature wrought,
Fair trees and gorgeous flowers;
The breezes their own languor lent;
The stars had feelings, which they sent
Into those favoured bowers.

Yet, in his worst pursuits, I ween
That sometimes there did intervene
Pure hopes of high intent:
For passions, linked to forms so fair
And stately, needs must have their share
Of noble sentiment.

But ill he lived, much evil saw,
With men to whom no better law
Nor better life was known ;
Deliberately, and undeceived,
Those wild men's vices he received,
And gave them back his own.

His genius and his moral frame
Were thus impaired, and he became
The slave of low desires :
A Man who without self-control
Would seek what the degraded soul
Unworthily admires.

And yet he with no feigned delight
Had wooed the Maiden, day and night
Had loved her, night and morn :
What could he less than love a Maid
Whose heart with so much nature played?
So kind and so forlorn !

Sometimes, most earnestly, he said,
'O Ruth ! I have been worse than dead ;
False thoughts, thoughts bold and vain,
Encompassed me on every side
When I, in confidence and pride,
Had crossed the Atlantic main.

' Before me shone a glorious world—
Fresh as a banner bright, unfurled
To music suddenly :
I looked upon those hills and plains,
And seemed as if let loose from chains,
To live at liberty.

'No more of this; for now, by thee,
Dear Ruth! more happily set free
With nobler zeal I burn;
My soul from darkness is released,
Like the whole sky when to the east
The morning doth return.'

Full soon that better mind was gone;
No hope, no wish remained, not one,—
They stirred him now no more;
New objects did new pleasure give,
And once again he wished to live
As lawless as before.

Meanwhile, as thus with him it fared,
They for the voyage were prepared,
And went to the seashore:
But, when they thither came, the Youth
Deserted his poor Bride, and Ruth
Could never find him more.

God help thee, Ruth!—Such pains she had,
That she in half a year was mad,
And in a prison housed;
And there, with many a doleful song
Made of wild words, her cup of wrong
She fearfully caroused.

Yet sometimes milder hours she knew,
Nor wanted sun, nor rain, nor dew,
Nor pastimes of the May;
—They all were with her in her cell;
And a clear brook with cheerful knell
Did o'er the pebbles play.

When Ruth three seasons thus had lain,
There came a respite to her pain;
She from her prison fled:
But of the Vagrant none took thought;
And where it liked her best she sought
Her shelter and her bread.

Among the fields she breathed again:
The master-current of her brain
Ran permanent and free;
And, coming to the Banks of Tone,
There did she rest; and dwell alone
Under the greenwood tree.

The engines of her pain, the tools
That shaped her sorrow, rocks and pools,
And airs that gently stir
The vernal leaves—she loved them still;
Nor ever taxed them with the ill
Which had been done to her.

A barn her *winter* bed supplies:
But, till the warmth of summer skies
And summer days is gone,
(And all do in this tale agree)
She sleeps beneath the greenwood tree,
And other home hath none.

An innocent life, yet far astray!
And Ruth will, long before her day,
Be broken down and old:
Sore aches she needs must have! but less
Of mind than body's wretchedness,
From damp, and rain, and cold.

If she is prest by want of food,
She from her dwelling in the wood
Repairs to a roadside ;
And there she begs at one steep place
Where up and down with easy pace
The horsemen-travellers ride.

That oaten pipe of hers is mute,
Or thrown away ; but with a flute
Her loneliness she cheers :
This flute, made of a hemlock stalk,
At evening in his homeward walk
The Quantock woodman hears.

I, too, have passed her on the hills
Setting her little water-mills
By spouts and fountains wild—
Such small machinery as she turned
Ere she had wept, ere she had mourned,
A young and happy Child !

Farewell ! and when thy days are told,
Ill-fated Ruth, in hallowed mould
Thy corpse shall buried be,
For thee a funeral bell shall ring,
And all the congregation sing
A Christian psalm for thee.

    1799.

RESOLUTION AND INDEPENDENCE

THERE was a roaring in the wind all night ;
    The rain came heavily and fell in floods ;
But now the sun is rising calm and bright ;
The birds are singing in the distant woods ;

Over his own sweet voice the Stock-dove broods ;
The Jay makes answer as the Magpie chatters ;
And all the air is filled with pleasant noise of waters.

All things that love the sun are out of doors ;
The sky rejoices in the morning's birth ;
The grass is bright with rain-drops ;—on the moors
The hare is running races in her mirth ;
And with her feet she from the plashy earth
Raises a mist ; that, glittering in the sun,
Runs with her all the way, wherever she doth run.

I was a Traveller then upon a moor,
I saw the hare that raced about with joy ;
I heard the woods and distant waters roar ;
Or heard them not, as happy as a boy :
The pleasant season did my heart employ :
My old remembrances went from me wholly ;
And all the ways of men, so vain and melancholy.

But, as it sometimes chanceth, from the might
Of joy in minds that can no further go,
As high as we have mounted in delight
In our dejection do we sink as low ;
To me that morning did it happen so :
And fears and fancies thick upon me came ;
Dim sadness—and blind thoughts, I knew not, nor
    could name.

I heard the sky-lark warbling in the sky ;
And I bethought me of the playful hare :
Even such a happy Child of earth am I ;
Even as these blissful creatures do I fare ;
Far from the world I walk, and from all care ;
But there may come another day to me—
Solitude, pain of heart, distress, and poverty.

My whole life I have lived in pleasant thought,
As if life's business were a summer mood;
As if all needful things would come unsought
To genial faith, still rich in genial good;
But how can He expect that others should
Build for him, sow for him, and at his call
Love him, who for himself will take no heed at all?

I thought of Chatterton, the marvellous Boy,
The sleepless Soul that perished in his pride;
Of Him who walked in glory and in joy
Following his plough, along the mountain-side:
By our own spirits are we deified:
We Poets in our youth begin in gladness;
But thereof come in the end despondency and madness.

Now, whether it were by peculiar grace,
A leading from above, a something given,
Yet it befell that, in this lonely place,
When I with these untoward thoughts had striven,
Beside a pool bare to the eye of heaven
I saw a Man before me unawares:
The oldest man he seemed that ever wore grey hairs.

As a huge stone is sometimes seen to lie
Couched on the bald top of an eminence;
Wonder to all who do the same espy,
By what means it could thither come, and whence;
So that it seems a thing endued with sense:
Like a sea beast crawled forth, that on a shelf
Of rock or sand reposeth, there to sun itself;

Such seemed this Man, not all alive nor dead,
Nor all asleep—in his extreme old age:
His body was bent double, feet and head
Coming together in life's pilgrimage;
As if some dire constraint of pain, or rage
Of sickness felt by him in times long past,
A more than human weight upon his frame had cast.

Himself he propped, limbs, body, and pale face,
Upon a long grey staff of shaven wood:
And, still as I drew near with gentle pace,
Upon the margin of that moorish flood
Motionless as a cloud the old Man stood,
That heareth not the loud winds when they call:
And moveth all together, if it move at all.

At length, himself unsettling, he the pond
Stirred with his staff, and fixedly did look
Upon the muddy water, which he conned,
As if he had been reading in a book;
And now a stranger's privilege I took;
And, drawing to his side, to him did say,
'This morning gives us promise of a glorious day.'

A gentle answer did the old Man make,
In courteous speech which forth he slowly drew:
And him with further words I thus bespake,
'What occupation do you there pursue?
This is a lonesome place for one like you.'
Ere he replied, a flash of mild surprise
Broke from the sable orbs of his yet-vivid eyes.

His words came feebly, from a feeble chest,
But each in solemn order followed each,
With something of a lofty utterance drest—
Choice word and measured phrase, above the reach
Of ordinary men; a stately speech;
Such as grave Livers do in Scotland use,
Religious men, who give to God and man their dues.

He told, that to these waters he had come
To gather leeches, being old and poor:
Employment hazardous and wearisome!
And he had many hardships to endure:
From pond to pond he roamed, from moor to moor;
Housing, with God's good help, by choice or chance;
And in this way he gained an honest maintenance.

The old Man still stood talking by my side;
But now his voice to me was like a stream
Scarce heard; nor word from word could I divide;
And the whole body of the Man did seem
Like one whom I had met with in a dream;
Or like a man from some far region sent,
To give me human strength, by apt admonishment.

My former thoughts returned: the fear that kills;
And hope that is unwilling to be fed;
Cold, pain, and labour, and all fleshly ills;
And mighty Poets in their misery dead.
—Perplexed, and longing to be comforted,
My question eagerly did I renew,
'How is it that you live, and what is it you do?'

He with a smile did then his words repeat;
And said, that, gathering leeches, far and wide

He travelled; stirring thus about his feet
The waters of the pools where they abide.
'Once I could meet with them on every side;
But they have dwindled long by slow decay;
Yet still I persevere, and find them where I may.'

While he was talking thus, the lonely place,
The old Man's shape, and speech—all troubled me:
In my mind's eye I seemed to see him pace
About the weary moors continually,
Wandering about alone and silently.
While I these thoughts within myself pursued,
He, having made a pause, the same discourse renewed.

And soon with this he other matter blended,
Cheerfully uttered, with demeanour kind,
But stately in the main; and when he ended,
I could have laughed myself to scorn to find
In that decrepit Man so firm a mind.
'God,' said I, 'be my help and stay secure;
I'll think of the Leech-gatherer on the lonely moor!'
    1807.

HART-LEAP WELL

Hart-Leap Well is a small spring of water, about five miles from
    Richmond, in Yorkshire, and near the side of the road that
    leads from Richmond to Askrigg. Its name is derived from a
    remarkable Chase, the memory of which is preserved by the
    monuments spoken of in the Second Part of the following
    poem, which monuments do now exist as I have there described
    them.

THE Knight had ridden down from Wensley Moor
    With the slow motion of a summer's cloud,
And now, as he approached a vassal's door,
'Bring forth another horse!' he cried aloud.

' Another horse ! '—That shout the vassal heard
And saddled his best Steed, a comely grey ;
Sir Walter mounted him ; he was the third
Which he had mounted on that glorious day.

Joy sparkled in the prancing courser's eyes ;
The horse and horseman are a happy pair :
But, though Sir Walter like a falcon flies,
There is a doleful silence in the air.

A rout this morning left Sir Walter's Hall,
That as they galloped made the echoes roar ;
But horse and man are vanished, one and all ;
Such race, I think, was never seen before.

Sir Walter, restless as a veering wind,
Calls to the few tired dogs that yet remain :
Blanch, Swift, and Music, noblest of their kind,
Follow, and up the weary mountain strain.

The Knight hallooed, he cheered and chid them on
With suppliant gestures and upbraidings stern ;
But breath and eyesight fail ; and, one by one,
The dogs are stretched among the mountain fern.

Where is the throng, the tumult of the race ?
The bugles that so joyfully were blown ?
—This chase it looks not like an earthly chase ;
Sir Walter and the Hart are left alone.

The poor Hart toils along the mountain-side ;
I will not stop to tell how far he fled,
Nor will I mention by what death he died ;
But now the Knight beholds him lying dead.

Dismounting, then, he leaned against a thorn;
He had no follower, dog, nor man, nor boy:
He neither cracked his whip, nor blew his horn,
But gazed upon the spoil with silent joy.

Close to the thorn on which Sir Walter leaned,
Stood his dumb partner in this glorious feat;
Weak as a lamb the hour that it is yeaned;
And white with foam as if with cleaving sleet.

Upon his side the Hart was lying stretched:
His nostril touched a spring beneath a hill,
And with the last deep groan his breath had fetched
The waters of the spring were trembling still.

And now, too happy for repose or rest
(Never had living man such joyful lot!),
Sir Walter walked all round, north, south, and west,
And gazed and gazed upon that darling spot.

And climbing up the hill—(it was at least
Four roods of sheer ascent) Sir Walter found
Three several hoof-marks which the hunted beast
Had left imprinted on the grassy ground.

Sir Walter wiped his face, and cried, 'Till now
Such sight was never seen by human eyes:
Three leaps have borne him from this lofty brow,
Down to the very fountain where he lies.

'I'll build a pleasure-house upon this spot,
And a small arbour, made for rural joy;
'Twill be the traveller's shed, the pilgrim's cot,
A place of love for damsels that are coy.

'A cunning artist will I have to frame
A basin for that fountain in the dell!
And they who do make mention of the same,
From this day forth, shall call it HART-LEAP WELL.

'And, gallant Stag! to make thy praises known,
Another monument shall here be raised;
Three several pillars, each a rough-hewn stone,
And planted where thy hoofs the turf have grazed.

'And, in the summer-time when days are long,
I will come hither with my paramour;
And with the dancers and the minstrel's song
We will make merry in that pleasant bower.

'Till the foundations of the mountains fail
My mansion with its arbour shall endure;—
The joy of them who till the fields of Swale,
And them who dwell among the woods of Ure!'

Then home he went, and left the Hart, stone-dead,
With breathless nostrils stretched above the spring.
—Soon did the Knight perform what he had said;
And far and wide the fame thereof did ring.

Ere thrice the Moon into her port had steered,
A cup of stone received the living well:
Three pillars of rude stone Sir Walter reared,
And built a house of pleasure in the dell.

And near the fountain, flowers of stature tall
With trailing plants and trees were intertwined,—
Which soon composed a little sylvan hall,
A leafy shelter from the sun and wind.

And thither, when the summer days were long,
Sir Walter led his wondering Paramour;
And with the dancers and the minstrel's song
Made merriment within that pleasant bower.

The Knight, Sir Walter, died in course of time,
 And his bones lie in his paternal vale.—
But there is matter for a second rhyme,
And I to this would add another tale.

PART SECOND

The moving accident is not my trade;
To freeze the blood I have no ready arts:
'Tis my delight, alone in summer shade,
To pipe a simple song for thinking hearts.

As I from Hawes to Richmond did repair,
It chanced that I saw standing in a dell
Three aspens at three corners of a square;
And one, not four yards distant, near a well.

What this imported I could ill divine:
And, pulling now the rein my horse to stop,
I saw three pillars standing in a line,—
The last stone-pillar on a dark hill-top.

The trees were grey, with neither arms nor head;
Half wasted the square mound of tawny green;
So that you just might say, as then I said,
'Here in old time the hand of man hath been.'

I looked upon the hill both far and near,
More doleful place did never eye survey;
It seemed as if the spring-time came not here,
And Nature here were willing to decay.

I stood in various thoughts and fancies lost,
When one, who was in shepherd's garb attired,
Came up the hollow:—him did I accost,
And what this place might be I then inquired.

The Shepherd stopped, and that same story told
Which in my former rhyme I have rehearsed.
'A jolly place,' said he, 'in times of old!
But something ails it now: the spot is curst.

'You see these lifeless stumps of aspen wood—
Some say that they are beeches, others elms—
These were the bower; and here a mansion stood,
The finest palace of a hundred realms!

'The arbour does its own condition tell;
You see the stones, the fountain, and the stream;
But as to the great Lodge! you might as well
Hunt half a day for a forgotten dream.

'There's neither dog nor heifer, horse nor sheep,
Will wet his lips within that cup of stone;
And oftentimes, when all are fast asleep,
This water doth send forth a dolorous groan.

'Some say that here a murder has been done,
And blood cries out for blood: but, for my part,
I've guessed, when I've been sitting in the sun,
That it was all for that unhappy Hart.

'What thoughts must through the creature's brain
        have passed!
Even from the topmost stone, upon the steep,
Are but three bounds—and look, Sir, at this last—
O Master! it has been a cruel leap.

'For thirteen hours he ran a desperate race;
And in my simple mind we cannot tell
What cause the Hart might have to love this place,
And come and make his death-bed near the well.

'Here on the grass, perhaps, asleep he sank,
Lulled by the fountain in the summer-tide;
This water was perhaps the first he drank
When he had wandered from his mother's side.

'In April here beneath the flowering thorn
He heard the birds their morning carols sing;
And he, perhaps, for aught we know, was born
Not half a furlong from that self-same spring

'Now, here is neither grass nor pleasant shade;
The sun on drearier hollow never shone;
So will it be, as I have often said,
Till trees, and stones, and fountains, all are gone.'

'Grey-headed Shepherd, thou hast spoken well;
Small difference lies between thy creed and mine:
This Beast not unobserved by Nature fell;
His death was mourned by sympathy divine.

  The Being, that is in the clouds and air,
That is in the green leaves among the groves,
Maintains a deep and reverential care
For the unoffending creatures whom He loves.

'The pleasure-house is dust :—behind, before,
This is no common waste, no common gloom;
But Nature, in due course of time, once more
Shall here put on her beauty and her bloom.

'She leaves these objects to a slow decay,
That what we are, and have been, may be known;
But at the coming of the milder day,
These monuments shall be all overgrown.

'One lesson, Shepherd, let us two divide,
Taught both by what she shows, and what conceals;
Never to bend our pleasure or our pride
With sorrow of the meanest thing that feels.'

   1800.

SONG AT THE FEAST OF BROUGHAM CASTLE

UPON THE RESTORATION OF LORD CLIFFORD, THE
SHEPHERD, TO THE ESTATES AND HONOURS OF
HIS ANCESTORS

HIGH in the breathless Hall the Minstrel sate,
     And Emont's murmur mingled with the
Song.—
The words of ancient time I thus translate,
A festal strain that hath been silent long:—

     'From town to town, from tower to tower,
The red rose is a gladsome flower.
Her thirty years of winter past,
The red rose is revived at last;
She lifts her head for endless spring,
For everlasting blossoming:
Both roses flourish, red and white:
In love and sisterly delight

The two that were at strife are blended,
And all old troubles now are ended.—
Joy ! joy to both ! but most to her
Who is the flower of Lancaster !
Behold her how She smiles to-day
On this great throng, this bright array !
Fair greeting doth she send to all
From every corner of the hall ;
But chiefly from above the board
Where sits in state our rightful lord,
A Clifford to his own restored !

    ' They came with banner, spear, and shield ;
And it was proved in Bosworth field.
Not long the Avenger was withstood—
Earth helped him with the cry of blood :
St. George was for us, and the might
Of blessed Angels crowned the right.
Loud voice the Land has uttered forth,
We loudest in the faithful north :
Our fields rejoice, our mountains ring,
Our streams proclaim a welcoming ;
Our strong abodes and castles see
The glory of their loyalty.

    ' How glad is Skipton at this hour—
Though lonely, a deserted Tower ;
Knight, squire, and yeoman, page and groom :
We have them at the feast of Brough'm.
How glad Pendragon—though the sleep
Of years be on her !—She shall reap
A taste of this great pleasure, viewing
As in a dream her own renewing.

Rejoiced is Brough, right glad I deem
Beside her little humble stream ;
And she that keepeth watch and ward
Her statelier Eden's course to guard ;
They both are happy at this hour,
Though each is but a lonely Tower :—
But here is perfect joy and pride
For one fair House by Emont's side,
This day, distinguished without peer
To see her Master and to cheer
Him, and his Lady-mother dear !

'Oh ! it was a time forlorn
When the fatherless was born—
Give her wings that she may fly,
Or she sees her infant die !
Swords that are with slaughter wild
Hunt the Mother and the Child.
Who will take them from the light ?
—Yonder is a man in sight—
Yonder is a house—but where ?
No, they must not enter there.
To the caves, and to the brooks,
To the clouds of heaven she looks ;
She is speechless, but her eyes
Pray in ghostly agonies.
Blissful Mary, Mother mild,
Maid and Mother undefiled,
Save a Mother and her Child !

'Now Who is he that bounds with joy
On Carrock's side, a Shepherd-boy ?

No thoughts hath he but thoughts that pass
Light as the wind along the grass.
Can this be He who hither came
In secret, like a smothered flame?
O'er whom such thankful tears were shed
For shelter, and a poor man's bread!
God loves the Child; and God hath willed
That those dear words should be fulfilled,
The Lady's words, when forced away
The last she to her Babe did say:
"My own, my own, thy Fellow-guest
I may not be; but rest thee, rest,
For lowly shepherd's life is best!"

Alas! when evil men are strong
No life is good, no pleasure long,
The Boy must part from Mosedale's groves,
And leave Blencathara's rugged coves,
And quit the flowers that summer brings
To Glenderamakin's lofty springs;
Must vanish, and his careless cheer
Be turned to heaviness and fear.
—Give Sir Lancelot Threlkeld praise!
Hear it, good man, old in days!
Thou tree of covert and of rest
For this young Bird that is distrest;
Among thy branches safe he lay,
And he was free to sport and play,
When falcons were abroad for prey.

'A recreant harp, that sings of fear
And heaviness in Clifford's ear!

I said, when evil men are strong,
No life is good, no pleasure long,
A weak and cowardly untruth!
Our Clifford was a happy Youth,
And thankful through a weary time,
That brought him up to manhood's prime.
—Again he wanders forth at will,
And tends a flock from hill to hill:
His garb is humble; ne'er was seen
Such garb with such a noble mien;
Among the shepherd grooms no mate
Hath he, a Child of strength and state!
Yet lacks not friends for simple glee,
Nor yet for higher sympathy.
To his side the fallow deer
Came, and rested without fear;
The eagle, lord of land and sea,
Stooped down to pay him fealty;
And both the undying fish that swim
Through Bowscale Tarn did wait on him;
The pair were servants of his eye
In their immortality;
And glancing, gleaming, dark or bright,
Moved to and fro, for his delight.
He knew the rocks which Angels haunt
Upon the mountains visitant;
He hath kenned them taking wing:
And into caves where Faeries sing
He hath entered; and been told
By Voices how men lived of old.
Among the heavens his eye can see
The face of thing that is to be;
And, if that men report him right,
His tongue could whisper words of might.

—Now another day is come,
Fitter hope, and nobler doom;
He hath thrown aside his crook,
And hath buried deep his book;
Armour rusting in his halls
On the blood of Clifford calls;—
" Quell the Scot," exclaims the Lance—
" Bear me to the heart of France,"
Is the longing of the Shield—
Tell thy name, thou trembling Field!
Field of death, where'er thou be,
Groan thou with our victory!
Happy day, and mighty hour,
When our Shepherd, in his power,
Mailed and horsed, with lance and sword,
To his ancestors restored
Like a reappearing Star,
Like a glory from afar,
First shall head the flock of war!'

Alas! the impassioned minstrel did not know
How, by Heaven's grace, this Clifford's heart was
      framed:
How he, long forced in humble walks to go,
Was softened into feeling, soothed, and tamed.

Love had he found in huts where poor men lie;
His daily teachers had been woods and rills,
The silence that is in the starry sky,
The sleep that is among the lonely hills.

In him the savage virtue of the Race,
Revenge, and all ferocious thoughts were dead:
Nor did he change; but kept in lofty place
The wisdom which adversity had bred.

Glad were the vales, and every cottage hearth;
The Shepherd-lord was honoured more and more;
And, ages after he was laid in earth,
'The good Lord Clifford' was the name he bore.

   1807.

LINES

COMPOSED A FEW MILES ABOVE TINTERN ABBEY, ON
   REVISITING THE BANKS OF THE WYE DURING
   A TOUR

JULY 13, 1798

FIVE years have passed; five summers, with the
    length
Of five long winters! and again I hear
These waters, rolling from their mountain springs
With a soft inland murmur.—Once again
Do I behold these steep and lofty cliffs,
That on a wild secluded scene impress
Thoughts of more deep seclusion; and connect
The landscape with the quiet of the sky.
The day is come when I again repose
Here, under this dark sycamore, and view
These plots of cottage ground, these orchard tufts,
Which at this season, with their unripe fruits,
Are clad in one green hue, and lose themselves
'Mid groves and copses.   Once again I see
These hedge-rows, hardly hedge-rows, little lines
Of sportive wood run wild: these pastoral farms,
Green to the very door; and wreaths of smoke
Sent up, in silence, from among the trees!
With some uncertain notice, as might seem

Of vagrant dwellers in the houseless woods,
Or of some Hermit's cave, where by his fire
The Hermit sits alone.
                              These beauteous forms,
Through a long absence, have not been to me
As is a landscape to a blind man's eye:
But oft, in lonely rooms, and 'mid the din
Of towns and cities, I have owed to them,
In hours of weariness, sensations sweet,
Felt in the blood, and felt along the heart;
And passing even into my purer mind,
With tranquil restoration :—feelings too
Of unremembered pleasure : such, perhaps,
As have no slight or trivial influence
On that best portion of a good's man's life,
His little, nameless, unremembered acts
Of kindness and of love.   Nor less, I trust,
To them I may have owed another gift,
Of aspect more sublime ; that blessed mood,
In which the burthen of the mystery,
In which the heavy and the weary weight
Of all this unintelligible world
Is lightened :—that serene and blessed mood,
In which the affections gently lead us on,—
Until the breath of this corporeal frame
And even the motion of our human blood
Almost suspended, we are laid asleep
In body, and become a living soul :
While with an eye made quiet by the power
Of harmony, and the deep power of joy,
We see into the life of things.
                              If this
Be but a vain belief, yet, oh! how oft—

In darkness and amid the many shapes
Of joyless daylight; when the fretful stir
Unprofitable, and the fever of the world,
Have hung upon the beatings of my heart—
How oft, in spirit, have I turned to thee,
O sylvan Wye! thou wanderer thro' the woods,
How often has my spirit turned to thee!

And now, with gleams of half-extinguished thought,
With many recognitions dim and faint,
And somewhat of a sad perplexity,
The picture of the mind revives again:
While here I stand, not only with the sense
Of present pleasure, but with pleasing thoughts
That in this moment there is life and food
For future years.   And so I dare to hope,
Though changed, no doubt, from what I was when
    first
I came among these hills; when like a roe
I bounded o'er the mountains by the sides
Of the deep rivers, and the lonely streams,
Wherever Nature led: more like a man
Flying from something that he dreads, than one
Who sought the thing he loved.   For Nature then
(The coarser pleasures of my boyish days,
And their glad animal movements all gone by)
To me was all in all.—I cannot paint
What then I was.   The sounding cataract
Haunted me like a passion: the tall rock,
The mountain, and the deep and gloomy wood,
Their colours and their forms, were then to me
An appetite; a feeling and a love,
That had no need of a remoter charm,

By thought supplied, nor any interest
Unborrowed from the eye.—That time is past,
And all its aching joys are now no more,
And all its dizzy raptures.   Not for this
Faint I, nor mourn nor murmur ; other gifts
Have followed ; for such loss, I would believe,
Abundant recompense.   For I have learned
To look on Nature, not as in the hour
Of thoughtless youth ; but hearing oftentimes
The still, sad music of humanity,
Nor harsh nor grating, though of ample power
To chasten and subdue.   And I have felt
A presence that disturbs me with the joy
Of elevated thoughts ; a sense sublime
Of something far more deeply interfused,
Whose dwelling is the light of setting suns,
And the round ocean and the living air,
And the blue sky, and in the mind of man :
A motion and a spirit, that impels
All thinking things, all objects of all thought,
And rolls through all things.   Therefore am I still
A lover of the meadows and the woods,
And mountains ; and of all that we behold
From this green earth ; of all the mighty world
Of eye, and ear,—both what they half create,
And what perceive ; well pleased to recognise
In nature and the language of the sense,
The anchor of my purest thoughts, the nurse,
The guide, the guardian of my heart, and soul
Of all my moral being.

                              Nor perchance,
If I were not thus taught, should I the more
Suffer my genial spirits to decay ;

For thou art with me here upon the banks
Of this fair river; thou, my dearest Friend,
My dear, dear Friend; and in thy voice I catch
The language of my former heart, and read
My former pleasures in the shooting lights
Of thy wild eyes.   Oh! yet a little while
May I behold in thee what I was once,
My dear, dear Sister! and this prayer I make
Knowing that Nature never did betray
The heart that loved her; 'tis her privilege
Through all the years of this our life, to lead
From joy to joy: for she can so inform
The mind that is within us, so impress
With quietness and beauty, and so feed
With lofty thoughts, that neither evil tongues,
Rash judgments, nor the sneers of selfish men,
Nor greetings where no kindness is, nor all
The dreary intercourse of daily life,
Shall e'er prevail against us, or disturb
Our cheerful faith that all which we behold
Is full of blessings.   Therefore let the moon
Shine on thee in thy solitary walk;
And let the misty mountain winds be free
To blow against thee: and, in after years,
When these wild ecstasies shall be matured
Into a sober pleasure; when thy mind
Shall be a mansion for all lovely forms,
Thy memory be as a dwelling-place
For all sweet sounds and harmonies; oh! then,
If solitude, or fear, or pain, or grief,
Should be thy portion, with what healing thoughts
Of tender joy wilt thou remember me,
And these my exhortations!   Nor, perchance—

If I should be where I no more can hear
Thy voice, nor catch from thy wild eyes these gleams
Of past existence—wilt thou then forget
That on the banks of this delightful stream
We stood together; and that I, so long
A worshipper of Nature, hither came
Unwearied in that service: rather say
With warmer love—oh! with far deeper zeal
Of holier love.   Nor wilt thou then forget,
That after many wanderings, many years
Of absence, these steep woods and lofty cliffs,
And this green pastoral landscape, were to me
More dear, both for themselves and for thy sake!

   1798.

FRENCH REVOLUTION

AS IT APPEARED TO ENTHUSIASTS AT ITS COMMENCEMENT

OH! pleasant exercise of hope and joy!
      For mighty were the auxiliars which then stood
Upon our side, we who were strong in love!
Bliss was it in that dawn to be alive,
But to be young was very heaven!—Oh! times
In which the meagre, stale, forbidding ways
Of custom, law, and statute, took at once
The attraction of a country in romance!
When Reason seemed the most to assert her rights,
When most intent on making of herself
A prime Enchantress—to assist the work
Which then was going forward in her name!

Not favoured spots alone, but the whole earth,
The beauty wore of promise, that which sets
(As at some moment might not be unfelt
Among the bowers of paradise itself)
The budding rose above the rose full blown.
What temper at the prospect did not wake
To happiness unthought of?   The inert
Were roused, and lively natures rapt away!
They who had fed their childhood upon dreams,
The playfellows of fancy, who had made
All powers of swiftness, subtilty, and strength
Their ministers,—who in lordly wise had stirred
Among the grandest objects of the sense,
And dealt with whatsoever they found there
As if they had within some lurking right
To wield it;—they, too, who, of gentle mood,
Had watched all gentle motions, and to these
Had fitted their own thoughts, schemers more mild,
And in the region of their peaceful selves;—
Now was it that both found, the meek and lofty
Did both find, helpers to their heart's desire,
And stuff at hand, plastic as they could wish;
Were called upon to exercise their skill,
Not in Utopia, subterranean fields,
Or some secreted island, Heaven knows where!
But in the very world which is the world
Of all of us,—the place where in the end
We find our happiness, or not at all!

    1805.

THE MOUNTAIN ECHO

YES, it was the mountain Echo,
    Solitary, clear, profound,
Answering to the shouting Cuckoo,
Giving to her sound for sound !

Unsolicited reply
To a babbling wanderer sent ;
Like her ordinary cry,
Like—but oh, how different !

Hears not also mortal Life ?
Hear not we, unthinking Creatures !
Slaves of folly, love, or strife—
Voices of two different natures ?

Have not *we* too ?—yes, we have
Answers, and we know not whence ;
Echoes from beyond the grave,
Recognised intelligence !

Such rebounds our inward ear
Catches sometimes from afar—
Listen, ponder, hold them dear ;
For of God,—of God they are.
    1806.

TO A SKY-LARK

ETHEREAL minstrel! pilgrim of the sky!
  Dost thou despise the earth where cares
  abound?
Or, while the wings aspire, are heart and eye
Both with thy nest upon the dewy ground?
Thy nest which thou canst drop into at will,
Those quivering wings composed, that music still!

Leave to the nightingale her shady wood;
A privacy of glorious light is thine;
Whence thou dost pour upon the world a flood
Of harmony, with instinct more divine;
Type of the wise who soar, but never roam:
True to the kindred points of Heaven and Home!

  1825.

LAODAMIA

'WITH sacrifice before the rising morn
  Vows have I made by fruitless hope inspired
And from the infernal Gods, 'mid shades forlorn
Of night, my slaughtered lord have I required:
Celestial pity I again implore;—
Restore him to my sight—great Jove, restore!'

So speaking, and by fervent love endowed
With faith, the suppliant heavenward lifts her hands;
While, like the sun emerging from a cloud,
Her countenance brightens—and her eye expands;
Her bosom heaves and spreads, her stature grows;
And she expects the issue in repose.

O terror! what hath she perceived?—O joy!
What doth she look on?—whom doth she behold?
Her hero slain upon the beach of Troy?
His vital presence? his corporeal mould?
It is—if sense deceive her not—'tis he!
And a god leads him, winged Mercury!

Mild Hermes spake—and touched her with his wand
That calms all fear: 'Such grace hath crowned thy
        prayer,
Laodamia! that at Jove's command
Thy Husband walks the paths of upper air:
He comes to tarry with thee three hours' space;
Accept the gift, behold him face to face!'

Forth sprang the impassioned Queen her Lord to
        clasp:
Again that consummation she essayed;
But unsubstantial form eludes her grasp
As often as that eager grasp was made.
The Phantom parts—but parts to reunite,
And reassume his place before her sight.

'Protesiláus, lo! thy guide is gone!
Confirm, I pray, the vision with thy voice:
This is our palace,—yonder is thy throne:
Speak, and the floor thou treadst on will rejoice.
Not to appal me have the gods bestowed
This precious boon; and blest a sad abode.'

'Great Jove, Laodamia! doth not leave
His gifts imperfect:—Spectre though I be,
I am not sent to scare thee or deceive;
But in reward of thy fidelity.
And something also did my worth obtain;
For fearless virtue bringeth boundless gain.

Thou knowest, the Delphic oracle foretold
That the first Greek who touched the Trojan strand
Should die : but me the threat could not withhold :
A generous cause a victim did demand ;
And forth I leapt upon the sandy plain ;
A self-devoted chief—by Hector slain.'

'Supreme of Heroes—bravest, noblest, best !
Thy matchless courage I bewail no more,
Which then, when tens of thousands were deprest
By doubt, propelled thee to the fatal shore ;
Thou found'st—and I forgive thee—here thou art—
A nobler counsellor than my poor heart.

' But thou, though capable of sternest deed,
Were kind as resolute, and good as brave ;
And he, whose power restores thee, hath decreed
Thou shouldst elude the malice of the grave ;
Redundant are thy locks, thy lips are fair
As when their breath enriched Thessalian air.

' No Spectre greets me—no vain Shadow this ;
Come, blooming Hero, place thee by my side !
Give, on this well-known couch, one nuptial kiss
To me, this day, a second time thy bride ! '
Jove frowned in heaven : the conscious Parcæ threw
Upon those roseate lips a Stygian hue.

' This visage tells thee that my doom is past :
Nor should the change be mourned, even if the joys
Of sense were able to return as fast
And surely as they vanish.   Earth destroys
Those raptures duly—Erebus disdains :
Calm pleasures there abide—majestic pains.

'Be taught, O faithful Consort, to control
Rebellious passion : for the Gods approve
The depth, and not the tumult, of the soul ;
A fervent, not ungovernable, love.
Thy transports moderate ; and meekly mourn
When I depart, for brief is my sojourn——'

'Ah, wherefore ?—Did not Hercules by force
Wrest from the guardian Monster of the tomb
Alcestis, a reanimated corse,
Given back to dwell on earth in vernal bloom ?
Medea's spells dispersed the weight of years.
And Æson stood a youth 'mid youthful peers.

'The Gods to us are merciful—and they
Yet further may relent ; for mightier far
Than strength of nerve and sinew, or the sway
Of magic potent over sun and star,
Is love, though oft to agony distrest,
And though his favourite seat be feeble woman's breast.

'But if thou goest, I follow——'   'Peace !' he said,—
She looked upon him and was calmed and cheered ;
The ghastly colour from his lips had fled ;
In his deportment, shape, and mien, appeared
Elysian beauty, melancholy grace,
Brought from a pensive though a happy place.

He spake of love, such love as Spirits feel
In worlds whose course is equable and pure ;
No fears to beat away—no strife to heal—
The past unsigh'd for, and the future sure ;
Spake of heroic arts in graver mood
Revived, with finer harmony pursued ;

Of all that is most beauteous—imaged there
In happier beauty : more pellucid streams,
An ampler ether, a diviner air,
And fields invested with purpureal gleams ;
Climes which the sun, who sheds the brightest day
Earth knows, is all unworthy to survey.

Yet there the Soul shall enter which hath earned
That privilege by virtue.—'Ill,' said he,
'The end of man's existence I discerned,
Who from ignoble games and revelry
Could draw, when we had parted, vain delight,
While tears were thy best pastime, day and night;

'And while my youthful peers before my eyes
(Each hero following his peculiar bent)
Prepared themselves for glorious enterprise
By martial sports,—or, seated in the tent,
Chieftains and kings in council were detained ;
What time the fleet at Aulis lay enchained.

'The wished-for wind was given :—I then revolved
The oracle, upon the silent sea ;
And, if no worthier led the way, resolved
That, of a thousand vessels, mine should be
The foremost prow in pressing to the strand,—
Mine the first blood that tinged the Trojan sand.

'Yet bitter, ofttimes bitter, was the pang
When of thy loss I thought, beloved Wife !
On thee too fondly did my memory hang,
And on the joys we shared in mortal life,—
The paths which we had trod—these fountains, flowers;
My new-planned cities, and unfinished towers.

'But should suspense permit the Foe to cry,
"Behold they tremble!—haughty their array,
Yet of their number no one dares to die"?
In soul I swept the indignity away:
Old frailties then recurred :—but lofty thought
In act embodied, my deliverance wrought.

'And Thou, though strong in love, art all too weak
In reason, in self-government too slow;
I counsel thee by fortitude to seek
Our blest reunion in the shades below.
The invisible world with thee hath sympathised;
Be thy affections raised and solemnised.

'Learn, by a mortal yearning, to ascend—
Seeking a higher object.   Love was given,
Encouraged, sanctioned, chiefly for that end;
For this the passion to excess was driven—
That self might be annulled: her bondage prove
The fetters of a dream, opposed to love.——'

Aloud she shrieked! for Hermes reappears!
Round the dear Shade she would have clung—'tis
    vain :
The hours are past—too brief had they been years;
And him no mortal effort can detain:
Swift, toward the realms that know not earthly day,
He through the portal takes his silent way,
And on the palace floor a lifeless corse She lay.

Thus, all in vain exhorted and reproved,
She perished; and, as for a wilful crime,
By the just Gods whom no weak pity moved,
Was doomed to wear out her appointed time,

Apart from happy Ghosts, that gather flowers
Of blissful quiet 'mid unfading bowers.

—Yet tears to human suffering are due;
And mortal hopes defeated and o'erthrown
Are mourned by man, and not by man alone,
As fondly he believes.—Upon the side
Of Hellespont (such faith was entertained)
A knot of spiry trees for ages grew
From out the tomb of him for whom she died:
And ever, when such stature they had gained
That Ilium's walls were subject to their view,
The trees' tall summits withered at the sight:
A constant interchange of growth and blight!

1814.

DION

See Plutarch

SERENE and fitted to embrace,
     Where'er he turned, a swan-like grace
Of haughtiness without pretence,
And to unfold a still magnificence,
Was princely Dion, in the power
And beauty of his happier hour.
And what pure homage *then* did wait
On Dion's virtues! while the lunar beam
Of Plato's genius, from its lofty sphere,
Fell round him in the grove of Academe,
Softening their inbred dignity austere—
     That he, not too elate
     With self-sufficing solitude,

But with majestic lowliness endued,
   Might in the universal bosom reign
And from affectionate observance gain
Help, under every change of adverse fate.

Five thousand warriors—Oh the rapturous day !
Each crowned with flowers, and armed with spear
      and shield,
Or ruder weapon which their course might yield,
To Syracuse advance in bright array.
Who leads them on ?—The anxious people see
Long-exiled Dion marching at their head,
He also crowned with flowers of Sicily,
And in a white, far-beaming, corselet clad !
Pure transport undisturbed by doubt or fear
The gazers feel ; and, rushing to the plain,
Salute those strangers as a holy train
Or blest the procession (to the immortals dear)
That brought their precious liberty again.
Lo ! when the gates are entered, on each hand,
Down the long street, rich goblets filled with wine
      In seemly order stand,
On tables set, as if for rites divine,—
And, as the great Deliverer marches by,
   He looks on festal ground with fruits bestrown ;
And flowers are on his person thrown
   In boundless prodigality :
Nor doth the general voice abstain from prayer
Invoking Dion's tutelary care,
As if a very Deity he were !

Mourn, hills and groves of Attica ! and mourn
Ilissus, bending o'er thy classic urn !

Mourn, and lament for him whose spirit dreads
Your once sweet memory, studious walks and
    shades
For him who to divinity aspired,
Not on the breath of popular applause,
But through dependence on the sacred laws
Framed in the schools where Wisdom dwelt retired,
Intent to trace the ideal path of right
(More fair than heaven's broad causeway paved with
    stars)
Which Dion learned to measure with sublime delight:
But he hath overleaped the eternal bars ;
And, following guides whose craft holds no consent
With aught that breathes the ethereal element,
Hath stained the robes of civil power with blood,
Unjustly shed, though for the public good,
Whence doubts that came too late, and wishes
    vain,
Hollow excuses, and triumphant pain ;
And oft his cogitations sink as low
As through the abysses of a joyless heart,
The heaviest plummet of despair can go—
But whence that sudden check ? that fearful start !
        He hears an uncouth sound—
        Anon his lifted eyes
Saw, at a long-drawn gallery's dusky bound,
A Shape of more than mortal size
And hideous aspect, stalking round and round.
        A woman's garb the Phantom wore,
        And fiercely swept the marble floor,—
        Like Auster whirling to and fro,
        His force on Caspian foam to try ;
Or Boreas when he scours the snow

That skins the plains of Thessaly,
Or when aloft on Mænalus he stops
His flight, 'mid eddying pine-tree tops!

So, but from toil less sign of profit reaping,
The sullen Spectre to her purpose bowed,
    Sweeping—vehemently sweeping—
No pause admitted, no design avowed!
' Avaunt, inexplicable Guest !—avaunt,'
Exclaimed the Chieftain—' let me rather see
The coronal that coiling vipers make,
The torch that flames with many a lurid flake,
And the long train of doleful pageantry
Which they behold, whom vengeful Furies haunt ;
Who, while they struggle from the scourge to flee,
Move where the blasted soil is not unworn,
And, in their anguish, bear what other minds have
    borne !'

But Shapes that come not at an earthly call,
Will not depart when mortal voices bid ;
Lords of the visionary eye whose lid,
Once raised, remains aghast, and will not fall!
Ye Gods, thought He, that servile Implement
Obeys a mystical intent :
Your Minister would brush away
The spots that to my soul adhere ;
But should she labour night and day,
They will not, cannot disappear ;
Whence angry perturbations,—and that look
Which no philosophy can brook !

Ill-fated Chief! there are whose hopes are built
Upon the ruins of thy glorious name ;

Who, through the portal of one moment's guilt,
Pursue thee with their deadly aim!
O matchless perfidy! portentous lust
Of monstrous crime!—that horror-striking blade,
Drawn in defiance of the Gods, hath laid
The noble Syracusan low in dust!
Shudder'd the walls—the marble city wept—
And sylvan places heaved a pensive sigh;
But in calm peace the appointed Victim slept,
As he had fallen in magnanimity;
Of spirit too capacious to require
That Destiny her course should change; too just
To his own native greatness to desire
That wretched boon, days lengthened by mistrust.
So were the hopeless troubles, that involved
The soul of Dion, instantly dissolved.
Released from life and cares of princely state,
He left this moral grafted on his Fate:
'Him only pleasure leads, and peace attends,
Him, only him, the shield of Jove defends,
Whose means are fair and spotless as his ends.'
1816

TO A YOUNG LADY

WHO HAD BEEN REPROACHED FOR TAKING LONG WALKS IN THE COUNTRY

DEAR Child of Nature, let them rail!
    —There is a nest in a green dale,
A harbour and a hold;
Where thou, a Wife and Friend, shalt see
Thy own heart-stirring days, and be
A light to young and old.

There, healthy as a shepherd boy,
And treading among flowers of joy
Which at no season fade,
Thou, while thy babes around thee cling,
Shalt show us how divine a thing
A Woman may be made.

Thy thoughts and feelings shall not die,
Nor leave thee, when grey hairs are nigh,
A melancholy slave;
But an old age serene and bright,
And lovely as a Lapland night,
Shall lead thee to thy grave.

   1803.

THE PRIMROSE OF THE ROCK

A ROCK there is whose homely front
   The passing traveller slights;
Yet there the glow-worms hang their lamps,
   Like stars, at various heights:
And one coy Primrose to that rock
   The vernal breeze invites.

What hideous warfare hath been waged,
   What kingdoms overthrown,
Since first I spied that primrose tuft
   And marked it for my own;
A lasting link in Nature's chain
   From highest heaven let down!

The flowers, still faithful to the stems,
    Their fellowship renew ;
The stems are faithful to the root,
    That worketh out of view ;
And to the rock the root adheres
    In every fibre true.

Close clings to earth the living rock,
    Though threatening still to fall ;
The earth is constant to her sphere ;
    And God upholds them all :
So blooms this lonely Plant, nor dreads
    Her annual funeral.

.   .   .   .   .

Here closed the meditative strain ;
    But air breathed soft that day,
The hoary mountain heights were cheered,
    The sunny vale looked gay,
And to the Primrose of the Rock
    I gave this after-lay.

I sang—Let myriads of bright flowers,
    Like Thee, in field and grove
Revive unenvied ;—mightier far,
    Than tremblings that reprove
Our vernal tendencies to hope,
    Is God's redeeming love ;

That love which changed—for wan disease,
    For sorrow that had bent
O'er hopeless dust, for withered age—
    Their moral element,
And turned the thistles of a curse
    To types beneficent.

Sin-blighted though we are, we too,
   The reasoning Sons of Men,
From one oblivious winter called
   Shall rise, and breathe again ;
And in eternal summer lose
   Our threescore years and ten.

To humbleness of heart descends
   This prescience from on high,
The faith that elevates the just,
   Before and when they die ;
And makes each soul a separate heaven
   A court for Deity.

     1831.

DEVOTIONAL INCITEMENTS

' Not to the earth confined,
Ascend to heaven.'

WHERE will they stop, those breathing powers,
   The Spirits of the new-born flowers ?
They wander with the breeze, they wind
Where'er the streams a passage find ;
Up from their native ground they rise
In mute aërial harmonies ;
From humble violet—modest thyme—
Exhaled, the essential odours climb,
As if no space below the sky
Their subtle flight could satisfy :
Heaven will not tax our thoughts with pride
If like ambition be *their* guide.

  Roused by this kindliest of May-showers,
The spirit-quickener of the flowers,

That with moist virtue softly cleaves
The buds, and freshens the young leaves.
The birds pour forth their souls in notes
Of rapture from a thousand throats—
Here checked by too impetuous haste,
While there the music runs to waste,
With bounty more and more enlarged,
Till the whole air is overcharged,
Give ear, O Man! to their appeal
And thirst for no inferior zeal,
Thou, who canst *think*, as well as feel.

Mount from the earth; aspire! aspire!
So pleads the town's cathedral quire,
In strains that from their solemn height
Sink, to attain a loftier flight;
While incense from the altar breathes
Rich fragrance in embodied wreaths;
Or, flung from swinging censer, shrouds
The taper-lights, and curls in clouds
Around angelic Forms, the still
Creation of the painter's skill,
That on the service wait concealed
One moment, and the next revealed
—Cast off your bonds, awake, arise,
And for no transient ecstasies!
What else can mean the visual plea
Of still or moving imagery—
The iterated summons loud,
Not wasted on the attendant crowd,
Nor wholly lost upon the throng
Hurrying the busy streets along?

Alas! the sanctities combined
By art to unsensualise the mind
Decay and languish; or, as creeds
And humours change, are spurned like weeds:
The priests are from their altars thrust;
Temples are levelled with the dust;
And solemn rites and awful forms
Founder amid fanatic storms.
Yet evermore, through years renewed
In undisturbed vicissitude
Of seasons balancing their flight
On the swift wings of day and night,
Kind Nature keeps a heavenly door
Wide open for the scattered poor
Where flower-breathed incense to the skies
Is wafted in mute harmonies;
And ground fresh cloven by the plough
Is fragrant with a humbler vow;
Where birds and brooks from leafy dells
Chime forth unwearied canticles,
And vapours magnify and spread
The glory of the sun's bright head—
Still constant in her worship, still
Conforming to the eternal Will,
Whether men sow or reap the fields,
Divine monition Nature yields,
That not by bread alone we live,
Or what a hand of flesh can give;
That every day should leave some part
Free for a sabbath of the heart:
So shall the seventh be truly blest,
From morn to eve, with hallowed rest.

    1832.

THE SONNET'S SCANTY PLOT

NUNS fret not at their convent's narrow room;
    And hermits are contented with their cells;
And students with their pensive citadels;
Maids at the wheel, the weaver at his loom,
Sit blithe and happy; bees that soar for bloom,
High as the highest peak of Furness Fells,
Will murmur by the hour in foxglove bells:
In truth the prison, unto which we doom
Ourselves, no prison is: and hence for me,
In sundry moods, 'twas pastime to be bound
Within the sonnet's scanty plot of ground;
Pleased if some souls (for such there needs must be)
Who have felt the weight of too much liberty,
Should find brief solace there, as I have found.

ADMONITION

Intended more particularly for the perusal of those who may have
    happened to be enamoured of some beautiful place of retreat,
    in the Country of the Lakes.

WELL may'st thou halt—and gaze with brighten-
    ing eye !
The lovely cottage in the guardian nook
Hath stirred thee deeply: with its own dear brook,
Its own small pasture, almost its own sky !
But covet not the abode :—forbear to sigh,
As many do, repining while they look;
Intruders—who would tear from Nature's book
This precious leaf, with harsh impiety.
Think what the home must be if it were thine,

Even thine, though few thy wants!—Roof, window,
    door,
The very flowers are sacred to the poor,
The roses to the porch which they entwine:
Yea, all, that now enchants thee, from the day
On which it should be touched, would melt away.

TO SLEEP

A FLOCK of sheep that leisurely pass by,
    One after one: the sound of rain, and bees
Murmuring; the fall of rivers, winds and seas,
Smooth fields, white sheets of water, and pure sky;
I have thought of all by turns, and yet do lie
Sleepless! and soon the small birds' melodies
Must hear, first uttered from my orchard trees;
And the first cuckoo's melancholy cry.
Even thus last night, and two nights more, I lay,
And could not win thee, Sleep! by any stealth:
So do not let me wear to-night away:
Without Thee what is all the morning's wealth?
Come, blessed barrier between day and day,
Dear mother of fresh thoughts and joyous health!

LONGING

SURPRISED by joy—impatient as the Wind
    I turned to share the transport—Oh! with whom
But Thee, deep buried in the silent tomb,
That spot which no vicissitude can find?
Love, faithful love, recalled thee to my mind—
But how could I forget thee? Through what power,
Even for the least division of an hour,

Have I been so beguiled as to be blind
To my most grievous loss ?—That thought's return
Was the worst pang that sorrow ever bore,
Save one, one only, when I stood forlorn,
Knowing my heart's best treasure was no more ;
That neither present time, nor years unborn
Could to my sight that heavenly face restore

THE VEILED THRONE

METHOUGHT I saw the footsteps of a throne
    Which mists and vapours from mine eyes did
    shroud—
Nor view of who might sit thereon allowed ;
But all the steps and ground about were strown
With sights the ruefullest that flesh and bone
Ever put on : a miserable crowd.
Sick, hale, old, young, who cried before that cloud,
'Thou art our king, O Death ! to thee we groan.'
Those steps I clomb ; the mists before me gave
Smooth way : and I beheld the face of one
Sleeping alone within a mossy cave,
With her face up to heaven ; that seemed to have
Pleasing remembrance of a thought foregone ;
A lovely Beauty in a summer grave !

THE INWARDNESS OF WORSHIP

IT is a beauteous evening, calm and free,
    The holy time is quiet as a Nun
Breathless with adoration ; the broad sun
Is sinking down in its tranquillity ;
The gentleness of heaven broods o'er the Sea :

Listen! the mighty Being is awake,
And doth with His eternal motion make
A sound like thunder—everlastingly.
Dear Child! dear Girl! that walkest with me here,
If thou appear untouched by solemn thought,
Thy nature is not therefore less divine:
Thou liest in Abraham's bosom all the year;
And worship'st at the Temple's inner shrine,
God being with thee when we know it not.

THE SHIP AND ITS DESTINATION

WHERE lies the Land to which yon Ship
  must go?
Fresh as a lark mounting at break of day,
Festively she puts forth in trim array;
Is she for tropic suns, or polar snow?
What boots the inquiry?—Neither friend nor foe
She cares for; let her travel where she may
She finds familiar names, a beaten way
Ever before her, and a wind to blow.
Yet still I ask, what haven is her mark?
And, almost as it was when ships were rare
(From time to time, like Pilgrims, here and there
Crossing the waters), doubt, and something dark,
Of the old Sea some reverential fear,
Is with me at thy farewell, joyous Bark!

THE WORLD AND OUR SPIRITS

THE world is too much with us; late and soon,
  Getting and spending, we lay waste our powers:
Little we see in Nature that is ours;

We have given our hearts away, a sordid boon !
This Sea that bares her bosom to the moon;
The winds that will be howling at all hours,
And are up-gathered now like sleeping flowers;
For this, for everything, we are out of tune;
It moves us not.—Great God! I'd rather be
A Pagan suckled in a creed outworn;
So might I, standing on this pleasant lea,
Have glimpses that would make me less forlorn·
Have sight of Proteus rising from the sea;
Or hear old Triton blow his wreathèd horn.

TO THE MEMORY OF RAISLEY
CALVERT

CALVERT! it must not be unheard by them
    Who may respect my name, that I to thee
Owed many years of early liberty.
This care was thine when sickness did condemn
Thy youth to hopeless wasting, root and stem—
That I, if frugal and severe, might stray
Where'er I liked: and finally array
My temples with the Muse's diadem.
Hence, if in freedom I have loved the truth;
If there be aught of pure, or good, or great,
In my past verse; or shall be, in the lays
Of higher mood which now I meditate;—
It gladdens me, O worthy, short-lived Youth!
To think how much of this will be thy praise.

THE SONNET

SCORN not the Sonnet; Critic, you have frowned,
　　Mindless of its just honours; with this key
Shakespeare unlocked his heart; the melody
Of this small lute gave ease to Petrarch's wound;
A thousand times this pipe did Tasso sound;
With it Camoens soothed an exile's grief;
The Sonnet glittered a gay myrtle leaf
Amid the cypress with which Dante crowned
His visionary brow: a glow-worm lamp,
It cheered mild Spenser, called from Faery-land
To struggle through dark ways; and, when a damp
Fell round the path of Milton, in his hand
The Thing became a trumpet; whence he blew
Soul-animating strains—alas, too few!

TO B. R. HAYDON

HIGH is our calling, Friend!—Creative Art
　　(Whether the instrument of words she use,
Or pencil pregnant with ethereal hues)
Demands the service of a mind and heart,
Though sensitive, yet, in their weakest part,
Heroically fashioned—to infuse
Faith in the whispers of the lonely Muse,
While the whole world seems adverse to desert.
And, oh! when Nature sinks, as oft she may,
Through long-lived pressure of obscure distress,
Still to be strenuous for the bright reward,
And in the soul admit of no decay,
Brook no continuance of weak-mindedness—
Great is the glory, for the strife is hard!

COMPOSED AFTER A JOURNEY

ACROSS THE HAMBLETON HILLS, YORKSHIRE

D ARK and more dark the shades of evening
          fell ;
The wished-for point was reached—but at an hour
When little could be gained from that rich dower
Of prospect, whereof many thousands tell.
Yet did the glowing west with marvellous power
Salute us ; there stood Indian citadel,
Temple of Greece, and minster with its tower
Substantially expressed—a place for bell
Or clock to toll from !   Many a tempting isle,
With groves that never were imagined, lay
'Mid seas how steadfast ! objects all for the eye
Of silent rapture ; but we felt the while
We should forget them ; they are of the sky,
And from our earthly memory fade away.

——'they are of the sky,
And from our earthly memory fade away.'

T HOSE words were uttered as in pensive mood
        We turned, departing from that solemn sight :
A contrast and reproach to gross delight,
And life's unspiritual pleasures daily wooed !
But now upon this thought I cannot brood ;
It is unstable as a dream of night ;
Nor will I praise a cloud, however bright,
Disparaging Man's gifts, and proper food.
Grove, isle, with every shape of sky-built dome,
Though clad in colours beautiful and pure,

Find in the heart of man no natural home :
The immortal Mind craves objects that endure :
These cleave to it ; from these it cannot roam,
Nor they from it : their fellowship is secure.

TO LADY BEAUMONT

LADY! the songs of Spring were in the grove
      While I was shaping beds for winter flowers ;
While I was planting green unfading bowers,
And shrubs—to hang upon the warm alcove,
And sheltering wall ; and still, as Fancy wove
The dream, to time and Nature's blended powers
I gave this paradise for winter hours,
A labyrinth, Lady! which your feet shall rove.
Yes! when the sun of life more feebly shines,
Becoming thoughts, I trust, of solemn gloom
Or of high gladness you shall hither bring ;
And these perennial bowers and murmuring pines
Be gracious as the music and the bloom
And all the mighty ravishment of spring.

TO A BROOK

BROOK! whose society the Poet seeks,
      Intent his wasted spirits to renew :
And whom the curious Painter doth pursue
Through rocky passes, among flowery creeks,
And tracks thee dancing down thy water-breaks ;
If wish were mine some type of thee to view,
Thee, and not thee thyself, I would not do
Like Grecian Artists, give thee human cheeks,
Channels for tears ; no Naiad shouldst thou be,—
Have neither limbs, feet, feathers, joints nor hairs :

It seems the Eternal Soul is clothed in thee
With purer robes than those of flesh and blood,
And hath bestowed on thee a safer good;
Unwearied joy, and life without its cares.

COMPOSED UPON WESTMINSTER BRIDGE
September 3, 1802

EARTH has not anything to show more fair:
　　Dull would he be of soul who could pass by
A sight so touching in its majesty:
This City now doth, like a garment, wear
The beauty of the morning: silent, bare,
Ships, towers, domes, theatres, and temples lie
Open unto the fields, and to the sky:
All bright and glittering in the smokeless air.
Never did sun more beautifully steep
In his first splendour, valley, rock, or hill:
Ne'er saw I, never felt, a calm so deep!
The river glideth at his own sweet will:
Dear God! the very houses seem asleep:
And all that mighty heart is lying still!

AT THE GRAVE OF BURNS
1803
SEVEN YEARS AFTER HIS DEATH

I SHIVER, Spirit fierce and bold,
　　At thought of what I now behold:
As vapours breathed from dungeons cold
　　　　Strike pleasure dead,
So sadness comes from out the mould
　　　　Where Burns is laid.

And have I then thy bones so near,
And thou forbidden to appear?
As if it were thyself that's here
    I shrink with pain;
And both my wishes and my fear
    Alike are vain.

Off weight—nor press on weight!—away
Dark thoughts!—they came, but not to stay;
With chastened feelings would I pay
    The tribute due
To him, and aught that hides his clay
    From mortal view.

Fresh as the flower, whose modest worth
He sang, his genius 'glinted' forth,
Rose like a star that touching earth,
    For so it seems,
Doth glorify its humble birth
    With matchless beams.

The piercing eye, the thoughtful brow,
The struggling heart, where be they now?—
Full soon the Aspirant of the plough,
    The prompt, the brave,
Slept, with the obscurest, in the low
    And silent grave.

I mourned with thousands, but as one
More deeply grieved, for He was gone
Whose light I hailed when first it shone,
    And showed my youth
How Verse may build a princely throne
    On humble truth.

Alas! where'er the current tends,
Regret pursues and with it blends,—
Huge Criffel's hoary top ascends
    By Skiddaw seen,—
Neighbours we were, and loving friends
    We might have been;

True friends though diversely inclined;
But heart with heart and mind with mind,
Where the main fibres are entwined,
    Through Nature's skill,
May even by contraries be joined
    More closely still.

The tear will start, and let it flow;
Thou 'poor Inhabitant below,'
At this dread moment—even so—
    Might we together
Have sate and talked where gowans blow,
    Or on wild heather.

What treasures would have then been placed
Within my reach; of knowledge graced
By fancy what a rich repast!
    But why go on?—
Oh! spare to sweep, thou mournful blast,
    His grave grass-grown.

There, too, a Son, his joy and pride
(Not three weeks past the Stripling died),
Lies gathered to his Father's side,
    Soul-moving sight!
Yet one to which is not denied
    Some sad delight.

For *he* is safe, a quiet bed
Hath early found among the dead,
Harboured where none can be misled,
    Wronged, or distrest;
And surely here it may be said
    That such are blest.

And oh for Thee, by pitying grace
Checked ofttimes in a devious race,
May He who halloweth the place
    Where Man is laid
Receive thy Spirit in the embrace
    For which it prayed!

Sighing I turned away; but ere
Night fell I heard, or seemed to hear,
Music that sorrow comes not near,
    A ritual hymn,
Chaunted in love that casts out fear
    By Seraphim.

THOUGHTS

SUGGESTED THE DAY FOLLOWING, ON THE BANKS
OF NITH, NEAR THE POET'S RESIDENCE

TOO frail to keep the lofty vow
    That must have followed when his brow
Was wreathed—'The Vision' tells us how—
    With holly spray,
He faltered, drifted to and fro,
    And passed away.

Well might such thoughts, dear Sister, throng
Our minds when, lingering all too long,
Over the grave of Burns we hung
    In social grief—
Indulged as if it were a wrong
    To seek relief.

But, leaving each unquiet theme
Where gentlest judgments may misdeem,
And prompt to welcome every gleam
    Of good and fair,
Let us beside this limpid Stream
    Breathe hopeful air.

Enough of sorrow, wreck, and blight;
Think rather of those moments bright
When to the consciousness of right
    His course was true,
When Wisdom prospered in his sight
    And virtue grew.

Yes, freely let our hearts expand,
Freely as in youth's season bland,
When side by side, his Book in hand,
    We wont to stray,
Our pleasure varying at command
    Of each sweet Lay.

How oft inspired must he have trode
These pathways, yon far-stretching road!
There lurks his home; in that Abode,
    With mirth elate,
Or in his nobly-pensive mood,
    The Rustic sate.

Proud thoughts that Image overawes,
Before it humbly let us pause,
And ask of Nature, from what cause
        And by what rules
She trained her Burns to win applause
        That shames the Schools.

Through busiest street and loneliest glen
Are felt the flashes of his pen ;
He rules mid winter snows, and when
        Bees fill their hives ;
Deep in the general heart of men
        His power survives.

What need of fields in some far clime
Where Heroes, Sages, Bards sublime,
And all that fetched the flowing rhyme
        From genuine springs,
Shall dwell together till old Time
        Folds up his wings ?

Sweet Mercy ! to the gates of Heaven
This Minstrel lead, his sins forgiven ;
The rueful conflict, the heart riven
        With vain endeavour,
And memory of Earth's bitter leaven
        Effaced for ever.

But why to Him confine the prayer,
When kindred thoughts and yearnings bear
On the frail heart the purest share
        With all that live ?—
The best of what we do and are,
        Just God, forgive !

TO A HIGHLAND GIRL

(AT INVERSNAID, UPON LOCH LOMOND)

SWEET Highland Girl, a very shower
   Of beauty is thy earthly dower!
Twice seven consenting years have shed
Their utmost bounty on thy head:
And these grey rocks; that household lawn;
Those trees, a veil just half withdrawn;
This fall of water that doth make
A murmur near the silent lake;
This little bay; a quiet road
That holds in shelter thy Abode—
In truth together do ye seem
Like something fashioned in a dream;
Such Forms as from their covert peep
When earthly cares are laid asleep!
But, O fair Creature! in the light
Of common day, so heavenly bright,
I bless Thee, Vision as thou art,
I bless thee with a human heart;
God shield thee to thy latest years!
Thee, neither know I, nor thy peers;
And yet my eyes are filled with tears.

With earnest feeling I shall pray
For thee when I am far away:
For never saw I mien, or face,
In which more plainly I could trace
Benignity and home-bred sense
Ripening in perfect innocence.
Here scattered, like a random seed,
Remote from men, thou dost not need

The embarrassed look of shy distress,
And maidenly shamefacedness :
Thou wear'st upon thy forehead clear
The freedom of a mountaineer :
A face with gladness overspread !
Soft smiles, by human kindness bred !
And seemliness complete, that sways
Thy courtesies, about thee plays ;
With no restraint, but such as springs
From quick and eager visitings
Of thoughts that lie beyond the reach
Of thy few words of English speech :
A bondage sweetly brooked, a strife
That gives thy gestures grace and life !
So have I, not unmoved in mind,
Seen birds of tempest-loving kind—
Thus beating up against the wind.

What hand but would a garland cull
For thee who art so beautiful ?
O happy pleasure ! here to dwell
Beside thee in some heathy dell ;
Adopt your homely ways and dress,
A Shepherd, thou a Shepherdess !
But I could frame a wish for thee
More like a grave reality :
Thou art to me but as a wave
Of the wild sea ; and I would have
Some claim upon thee, if I could,
Though but of common neighbourhood.
What joy to hear thee, and to see !
Thy elder Brother I would be,
Thy Father—anything to thee !

Now thanks to Heaven! that of its grace
Hath led me to this lonely place.
Joy have I had; and going hence
I bear away my recompense.
In spots like these it is we prize
Our Memory, feel that she hath eyes:
Then, why should I be loth to stir?
I feel this place was made for her:
To give new pleasure like the past,
Continued long as life shall last.
Nor am I loth, though pleased at heart,
Sweet Highland Girl! from thee to part;
For I, methinks, till I grow old,
As fair before me shall behold
As I do now the cabin small,
The lake, the bay, the waterfall;
And Thee, the Spirit of them all!

GLEN ALMAIN

OR, THE NARROW GLEN

IN this still place, remote from men,
    Sleeps Ossian, in the NARROW GLEN;
In this still place, where murmurs on
But one meek streamlet, only one:
He sang of battles, and the breath
Of stormy war, and violent death;
And should, methinks, when all was past,
Have rightfully been laid at last
Where rocks were rudely heaped, and rent
As by a spirit turbulent;
Where sights were rough, and sounds were wild,
And everything unreconciled;

In some complaining, dim retreat,
For fear and melancholy meet ;
But this is calm ; there cannot be
A more entire tranquillity.

Does then the Bard sleep here indeed ?
Or is it but a groundless creed ?
What matters it ?—I blame them not
Whose Fancy in this lonely Spot
Was moved ; and in such way expressed
Their notion of its perfect rest.
A convent, even a hermit's cell,
Would break the silence of this Dell :
It is not quiet, is not ease ;
But something deeper far than these :
The separation that is here
Is of the grave ; and of austere
Yet happy feelings of the dead :
And, therefore, was it rightly said
That Ossian, last of all his race !
Lies buried in this lonely place.

STEPPING WESTWARD

While my fellow-traveller and I were walking by the side of
Loch Ketterine (Katrine), one fine evening after sunset, in our
road to a hut where, in the course of our tour, we had been
hospitably entertained some weeks before, we met, in one of the
loneliest parts of that solitary region, two well-dressed women,
one of whom said to us, by way of greeting, ' What, you are
stepping westward ?'

' *WHAT, you are stepping westward ?*'—'*Yea.*'
    —'Twould be a *wildish* destiny,
If we, who thus together roam
In a strange Land, and far from home,

Were in this place the guests of Chance:
Yet who would stop, or fear to advance,
Though home or shelter he had none,
With such a sky to lead him on?

The dewy ground was dark and cold;
Behind, all gloomy to behold;
And stepping westward seemed to be
A kind of *heavenly* destiny:
I liked the greeting; 'twas a sound
Of something without place or bound;
And seemed to give me spiritual right
To travel through that region bright.

The voice was soft, and she who spake
Was walking by her native lake:
The salutation had to me
The very sound of courtesy:
Its power was felt; and while my eye
Was fixed upon the glowing Sky,
The echo of the voice enwrought
A human sweetness with the thought
Of travelling through the world that lay
Before me in my endless way.

THE SOLITARY REAPER

BEHOLD her, single in the field,
　　Yon solitary Highland Lass!
Reaping and singing by herself;
Stop here, or gently pass!

Alone she cuts and binds the grain,
And sings a melancholy strain;
O listen! for the Vale profound
Is overflowing with the sound.

No Nightingale did ever chaunt
More welcome notes to weary bands
Of travellers in some shady haunt,
Among Arabian sands;
A voice so thrilling ne'er was heard
In spring-time from the Cuckoo-bird,
Breaking the silence of the seas
Among the farthest Hebrides.

Will no one tell me what she sings?—
Perhaps the plaintive numbers flow
For old, unhappy, far-off things,
And battles long ago:
Or is it some more humble lay,
Familiar matter of to-day?
Some natural sorrow, loss, or pain,
That has been, and may be again?

Whate'er the theme, the Maiden sang
As if her song could have no ending;
I saw her singing at her work,
And o'er the sickle bending;—
I listened, motionless and still;
And, as I mounted up the hill,
The music in my heart I bore,
Long after it was heard no more.

ADDRESS

TO KILCHURN CASTLE, UPON LOCH AWE

From the top of the hill a most impressive scene opened upon
our view,—a ruined Castle on an Island (for an Island the
flood had made it) at some distance from the shore, backed
by a Cove of the Mountain Cruachan, down which came a
foaming stream. The Castle occupied every foot of the Island
that was visible to us, appearing to rise out of the water,—
mists rested upon the mountain side, with spots of sunshine ;
there was a mild desolation in the low grounds, a solemn
grandeur in the mountains, and the Castle was wild, yet
stately—not dismantled of turrets—nor the walls broken down,
though obviously a ruin.'—*Extract from the Journal of my
Companion.*

CHILD of loud-throated War ! the mountain
      Stream
Roars in thy hearing ; but thy hour of rest
Is come, and thou art silent in thy age ;
Save when the wind sweeps by and sounds are caught
Ambiguous, neither wholly thine nor theirs.
Oh ! there is life that breathes not ; Powers there are
That touch each other to the quick in modes
Which the gross world no sense hath to perceive,
No soul to dream of. What art Thou, from care
Cast off—abandoned by thy rugged Sire,
Nor by soft Peace adopted ; though, in place
And in dimension, such that thou might'st seem
But a mere footstool to yon sovereign Lord,.
Huge Cruachan (a thing that meaner hills
Might crush, nor know that it had suffered harm),
Yet he, not loth, in favour of thy claims
To reverence, suspends his own ; submitting
All that the God of Nature hath conferred,

All that he holds in common with the stars,
To the memorial majesty of Time
Impersonated in thy calm decay!

Take, then, thy seat, Vicegerent unreproved!
Now, while a farewell gleam of evening light
Is fondly lingering on thy shattered front,
Do thou, in turn, be paramount; and rule
Over the pomp and beauty of a scene
Whose mountains, torrents, lake, and woods, unite
To pay thee homage; and with these are joined,
In willing admiration and respect,
Two Hearts, which in thy presence might be called
Youthful as Spring.—Shade of departed Power,
Skeleton of unfleshed humanity,
The chronicle were welcome that should call
Into the compass of distinct regard
The toils and struggles of thy infant years!
Yon foaming flood seems motionless as ice;
Its dizzy turbulence eludes the eye,
Frozen by distance; so, majestic Pile,
To the perception of this Age, appear
Thy fierce beginnings, softened and subdued
And quieted in character—the strife,
The pride, the fury uncontrollable,
Lost on the aërial heights of the Crusades!

SONNET

COMPOSED AT —— CASTLE

DEGENERATE Douglas! oh, the unworthy Lord!
   Whom mere despite of heart could so far please,
And love of havoc (for with such disease
Fame taxes him), that he could send forth word

To level with the dust a noble horde,
A brotherhood of venerable Trees,
Leaving an ancient dome, and towers like these,
Beggared and outraged !—Many hearts deplored
The fate of those old Trees ; and oft with pain
The traveller, at this day, will stop and gaze
On wrongs, which Nature scarcely seems to heed :
For sheltered places, bosoms, nooks, and bays,
And the pure mountains, and the gentle Tweed,
And the green silent pastures, yet remain.

YARROW UNVISITED

(See the various Poems the scene of which is laid upon the banks of
the Yarrow ; in particular, the exquisite ballad of Hamilton
beginning

'Busk ye, busk ye, my bonny, bonny bride,
Busk ye, busk ye, my winsome marrow ! ')

FROM Stirling Castle we had seen
    The mazy Forth unravelled ;
Had trod the banks of Clyde, and Tay,
And with the Tweed had travelled ;
And when we came to Clovenford,
Then said my ' *winsome marrow*,'
'Whate'er betide, we'll turn aside,
And see the Braes of Yarrow.'

' Let Yarrow folk, *frae* Selkirk town,
Who have been buying, selling,
Go back to Yarrow, 'tis their own :
Each maiden to her dwelling !
On Yarrow's banks let herons feed,
Hares couch, and rabbits burrow !
But we will downward with the Tweed,
Nor turn aside to Yarrow.

'There's Gala Water, Leader Haughs,
Both lying right before us;
And Dryburgh, where with chiming Tweed
The lintwhites sing in chorus;
There's pleasant Teviot-dale, a land
Made blithe with plough and harrow:
Why throw away a needful day
To go in search of Yarrow?

'What's Yarrow but a river bare,
That glides the dark hills under?
There are a thousand such elsewhere
As worthy of your wonder.'
—Strange words they seemed of slight and
    scorn;
My True-love sighed for sorrow;
And looked me in the face, to think
I thus could speak of Yarrow!

'Oh! green,' said I, 'are Yarrow's holms,
And sweet is Yarrow flowing!
Fair hangs the apple frae the rock,[1]
But we will leave it growing.
O'er hilly path, and open Strath,
We'll wander Scotland thorough;
But, though so near, we will not turn
Into the dale of Yarrow.

'Let beeves and home-bred kine partake
The sweets of Burn Mill meadow;
The swan on still St. Mary's Lake
Float double, swan and shadow!

[1] See Hamilton's ballad as above.

We will not see them; will not go,
To-day, nor yet to-morrow;
Enough, if in our hearts we know
There's such a place as Yarrow.

' Be Yarrow stream unseen, unknown!
It must, or we shall rue it:
We have a vision of our own;
Ah! why should we undo it?
The treasured dreams of times long past,
We'll keep them, winsome Marrow!
For when we're there, although 'tis fair,
'Twill be another Yarrow!

'If Care with freezing years should come,
And wandering seem but folly,—
Should we be loth to stir from home,
And yet be melancholy;
Should life be dull, and spirits low,
'Twill soothe us in our sorrow,
That earth has something yet to show,
The bonny holms of Yarrow!'

SONNET

IN THE PASS OF KILLIECRANKIE

An invasion being expected, October 1803

SIX thousand veterans practised in war's game,
    Tried men, at Killiecrankie, were arrayed
Against an equal host that wore the plaid,
Shepherds and herdsmen.—Like a whirlwind came
The Highlanders, the slaughter spread like flame;

And Garry, thundering down his mountain-road,
Was stopped and could not breathe beneath the load
Of the dead bodies.—'Twas a day of shame
For them whom precept and the pedantry
Of cold mechanic battle do enslave.
O for a single hour of that Dundee
Who on that day the word of onset gave!
Like conquest would the Men of England see;
And her Foes find a like inglorious grave.

YARROW VISITED

SEPTEMBER 1814

AND is this—Yarrow?—*This* the Stream
    Of which my fancy cherished,
So faithfully, a waking dream?
An image that hath perished!
O that some Minstrel's harp were near,
To utter notes of gladness,
And chase this silence from the air,
That fills my heart with sadness!

Yet why?—a silvery current flows
With uncontrolled meanderings;
Nor have these eyes by greener hills
Been soothed, in all my wanderings.
And, through her depths, Saint Mary's Lake
Is visibly delighted;
For not a feature of those hills
Is in the mirror slighted.

A blue sky bends o'er Yarrow vale,
Save where that pearly whiteness
Is round the rising sun diffused,
A tender hazy brightness ;
Mild dawn of promise ! that excludes
All profitless dejection ;
Though not unwilling here to admit
A pensive recollection.

Where was it that the famous Flower
Of Yarrow Vale lay bleeding ?
His bed perchance was yon smooth mound
On which the herd is feeding :
And haply from this crystal pool,
Now peaceful as the morning,
The Water-wraith ascended thrice—
And gave his doleful warning.

Delicious is the Lay that sings
The haunts of happy Lovers,
The path that leads them to the grove,
The leafy grove that covers :
And Pity sanctifies the Verse
That paints, by strength of sorrow,
The unconquerable strength of love ;
Bear witness, rueful Yarrow !

But thou, that didst appear so fair
To fond imagination,
Dost rival in the light of day
Her delicate creation :
Meek loveliness is round thee spread,
A softness still and holy ;
The grace of forest charms decayed,
And pastoral melancholy.

That region left, the vale unfolds
Rich groves of lofty stature,
With Yarrow winding through the pomp
Of cultivated nature;
And, rising from those lofty groves,
Behold a Ruin hoary!
The shattered front of Newark's towers,
Renowned in Border story.

Fair scenes for childhood's opening bloom,
For sportive youth to stray in;
For manhood to enjoy his strength;
And age to wear away in!
Yon cottage seems a bower of bliss,
A covert for protection
Of tender thoughts, that nestle there—
The brood of chaste affection.

How sweet, on this autumnal day,
The wild-wood fruits to gather,
And on my True-love's forehead plant
A crest of blooming heather!
And what if I enwreathed my own!
'Twere no offence to reason;
The sober Hills thus deck their brows
To meet the wintry season.

I see—but not by sight alone,
Loved Yarrow, have I won thee;
A ray of fancy still survives—
Her sunshine plays upon thee!

Thy ever-youthful waters keep
A course of lively pleasure;
And gladsome notes my lips can breathe,
Accordant to the measure.

The vapours linger round the Heights,
They melt, and soon must vanish;
One hour is theirs, nor more is mine—
Sad thought, which I would banish,
But that I know, where'er I go,
Thy genuine image, Yarrow!
Will dwell with me—to heighten joy,
And cheer my mind in sorrow.

COMPOSED BY THE SEA-SIDE
NEAR CALAIS

AUGUST 1802

FAIR Star of evening, Splendour of the west,
    Star of my Country!—on the horizon's brink
Thou hangest, stooping, as might seem, to sink
On England's bosom; yet well pleased to rest,
Meanwhile, and be to her a glorious crest
Conspicuous to the Nations. Thou, I think,
Shouldst be my Country's emblem; and shouldst wink,
Bright Star! with laughter on her banners, drest
In thy fresh beauty. There! that dusky spot
Beneath thee, that is England; there she lies.
Blessings be on you both! one hope, one lot,
One life, one glory!—I, with many a fear
For my dear Country, many heartfelt sighs,
Among men who do not love her, linger here.

ON THE EXTINCTION OF THE VENETIAN REPUBLIC

ONCE did She hold the gorgeous East in fee;
And was the safeguard of the West; the
worth
Of Venice did not fall below her birth,
Venice, the eldest Child of Liberty,
She was a maiden City, bright and free;
No guile seduced, no force could violate;
And, when she took unto herself a Mate,
She must espouse the everlasting Sea.
And what if she had seen those glories fade,
Those titles vanish, and that strength decay;
Yet shall some tribute of regret be paid
When her long life hath reached its final day;
Men are we, and must grieve when even the
Shade
Of that which once was great is passed away.

TO TOUSSAINT L'OUVERTURE

TOUSSAINT, the most unhappy man of
men!
Whether the whistling Rustic tend his plough
Within thy hearing, or thy head be now
Pillowed in some deep dungeon's earless den;—
O miserable Chieftain! where and when
Wilt thou find patience? Yet die not: do thou
Wear rather in thy bonds a cheerful brow:
Though fallen thyself, never to rise again

Live, and take comfort.   Thou hast left behind
Powers that will work for thee ; air, earth, and skies ;
There's not a breathing of the common wind
That will forget thee ; thou hast great allies ;
Thy friends are exultations, agonies,
And love, and man's unconquerable mind.

NEAR DOVER
September 1802

INLAND, within a hollow vale, I stood ;
  And saw, while sea was calm and air was clear,
The coast of France—the coast of France how near !
Drawn almost into frightful neighbourhood.
I shrunk ; for verily the barrier flood
Was like a lake, or river bright and fair,
A span of waters ; yet what power is there !
What mightiness for evil and for good !
Even so doth God protect us if we be
Virtuous and wise.   Winds blow, and waters roll,
Strength to the brave, and Power, and Deity ;
Yet in themselves are nothing !   One decree
Spake laws to *them*, and said that by the soul
Only, the Nations shall be great and free.

THOUGHT OF A BRITON ON THE SUBJUGATION OF SWITZERLAND

TWO Voices are there ; one is of the sea,
  One of the mountains ; each a mighty Voice :
In both from age to age thou didst rejoice,
They were thy chosen music, Liberty !

There came a Tyrant, and with holy glee
Thou fought'st against him; but hast vainly
    striven:
Thou from thy Alpine holds at length art driven,
Where not a torrent murmurs heard by thee.
Of one deep bliss thine ear hath been bereft:
Then cleave, O cleave to that which still is left;
For, high-souled Maid, what sorrow would it be
That Mountain floods should thunder as before,
And Ocean bellow from his rocky shore,
And neither awful Voice be heard by thee!

WRITTEN IN LONDON

SEPTEMBER 1802

O FRIEND! I know not which way I must
    look
For comfort, being, as I am, opprest.
To think that now our life is only drest
For show; mean handiwork of craftsman, cook,
Or groom!—We must run glittering like a
    brook
In the open sunshine, or we are unblest;
The wealthiest man among us is the best:
No grandeur now in nature or in book
Delights us. Rapine, avarice, expense,
This is idolatry; and these we adore:
Plain living and high thinking are no more:
The homely beauty of the good old cause
Is gone; our peace, our fearful innocence,
And pure religion breathing household laws.

LONDON
1802

MILTON ! thou should'st be living at this hour:
    England hath need of thee : she is a fen
Of stagnant waters : altar, sword, and pen,
Fireside, the heroic wealth of hall and bower,
Have forfeited their ancient English dower
Of inward happiness.   We are selfish men ;
Oh ! raise us up, return to us again ;
And give us manners, virtue, freedom, power,
Thy soul was like a Star, and dwelt apart :
Thou hadst a voice whose sound was like the sea :
Pure as the naked heavens, majestic, free,
So didst thou travel on life's common way,
In cheerful godliness : and yet thy heart
The lowliest duties on herself did lay.

BRITONS AND FREEDOM

IT is not to be thought of that the Flood
    Of British freedom, which, to the open sea
Of the world's praise, from dark antiquity
Hath flowed, 'with pomp of waters, unwithstood,'
Roused though it be full often to a mood
Which spurns the check of salutary bands,
That this most famous Stream in bogs and sands
Should perish : and to evil and to good
Be lost for ever.   In our halls is hung
Armoury of the invincible Knights of old :
We must be free or die, who speak the tongue
That Shakspeare spake ; the faith and morals hold
Which Milton held.—In everything we are sprung
Of Earth's first blood, have titles manifold.

A BRITON'S LOVE FOR BRITAIN

WHEN I have borne in memory what has
        tamed
Great Nations, how ennobling thoughts depart
When men change swords for ledgers, and desert
The student's bower for gold, some fears un-
        named
I had, my Country!—am I to be blamed?
Now, when I think of thee, and what thou art,
Verily, in the bottom of my heart,
Of those unfilial fears I am ashamed,
For dearly must we prize thee; we who find
In thee a bulwark for the cause of men;
And I by my affection was beguiled:
What wonder if a Poet now and then,
Among the many movements of his mind,
Felt for thee as a lover or a child!

TO THE MEN OF KENT

OCTOBER 1803

VANGUARD of Liberty, ye men of Kent,
        Ye children of a Soil that doth advance
Her haughty brow against the coast of France,
Now is the time to prove your hardiment!
To France be words of invitation sent!
They from their fields can see the countenance
Of your fierce war, may ken the glittering lance,
And hear you shouting forth your brave intent.
Left single, in bold parley, ye, of yore,
Did from the Norman win a gallant wreath;

Confirmed the charters that were yours before;—
No parleying now! In Britain is one breath;
We all are with you now from shore to shore:—
Ye men of Kent, 'tis victory or death!

THE CONVENTION OF CINTRA

COMPOSED WHILE THE AUTHOR WAS ENGAGED IN WRITING A TRACT OCCASIONED BY IT

1808

NOT 'mid the World's vain objects that enslave
　　The free-born Soul—that World whose vaunted
skill
In selfish interest perverts the will,
Whose factions lead astray the wise and brave—
Not there; but in dark wood and rocky cave,
And hollow vale which foaming torrents fill
With omnipresent murmur as they rave
Down their steep beds, that never shall be still;
Here, mighty Nature; in this school sublime
I weigh the hopes and fears of suffering Spain;
For her consult the auguries of time,
And through the human heart explore my way:
And look and listen—gathering, whence I may,
Triumph, and thoughts no bondage can restrain.

1811

THE power of Armies is a visible thing,
　　Formal, and circumscribed in time and space;
But who the limits of that power shall trace
Which a brave People into light can bring
Or hide, at will,—for freedom combating

By just revenge inflamed? No foot may chase,
No eye can follow, to a fatal place
That power, that spirit, whether on the wing
Like the strong wind, or sleeping like the wind
Within its awful caves.—From year to year
Springs this indigenous produce far and near;
No craft this subtle element can bind,
Rising like water from the soil, to find
In every nook a lip that it may cheer.

THE PINE OF MONTE MARIO AT ROME

I SAW far off the dark top of a Pine
   Look like a cloud—a slender stem the tie
That bound it to its native earth—poised high
'Mid evening hues, along the horizon line,
Striving in peace each other to outshine.
But when I learned the Tree was living there
Saved from the sordid axe by Beaumont's care,
Oh, what a gush of tenderness was mine!
The rescued Pine-tree, with its sky so bright
And cloud-like beauty, rich in thoughts of home,
Death-parted friends, and days too swift in flight,
Supplanted the whole majesty of Rome
(Then first apparent from the Pincian Height)
Crowned with St. Peter's everlasting Dome.

INSIDE OF KING'S COLLEGE CHAPEL, CAMBRIDGE

TAX not the royal Saint with vain expense,
   With ill-matched aims the Architect who planned—
Albeit labouring for a scanty band
Of white-robed Scholars only—this immense

And glorious Work of fine intelligence !
Give all thou canst ; high Heaven rejects the lore
Of nicely-calculated less or more ;
So deemed the man who fashioned for the sense
These lofty pillars, spread that branching roof
Self-poised, and scooped into ten thousand cells,
Where light and shade repose, where music dwells
Lingering—and wandering on as loth to die ;
Like thoughts whose very sweetness yieldeth proof
That they were born for immortality.

YARROW REVISITED

[The following Stanzas are a memorial of a day passed with Sir
    Walter Scott, and other Friends visiting the Banks of the
    Yarrow under his guidance, immediately before his departure
    from Abbotsford for Naples (1831).
      The title *Yarrow Revisited* will stand in no need of explana-
    tion, for Readers acquainted with the Author's previous poems
    suggested by that celebrated Stream.]

THE gallant Youth, who may have gained,
    Or seeks, a ' winsome Marrow,'
Was but an Infant in the lap
    When first I looked on Yarrow ;
Once more, by Newark's Castle-gate
    Long left without a warder,
I stood, looked, listened, and with Thee,
    Great Minstrel of the Border !

Grave thoughts ruled wide on that sweet day,
    Their dignity installing
In gentle bosoms, while sere leaves
    Were on the bough, or falling ;

But breezes played, and sunshine gleamed—
  The forest to embolden;
Reddened the fiery hues, and shot
  Transparence through the golden.

For busy thoughts the Stream flowed on
  In foamy agitation;
And slept in many a crystal pool
  For quiet contemplation:
No public and no private care
  The freeborn mind enthralling:
We made a day of happy hours,
  Our happy days recalling.

Brisk Youth appeared, the Morn of youth,
  With freaks of graceful folly,—
Life's temperate Noon, her sober Eve,
  Her Night not melancholy;
Past, present, future, all appeared
  In harmony united,
Like guests that meet, and some from far,
  By cordial love invited.

And if, as Yarrow, through the woods
  And down the meadow ranging,
Did meet us with unaltered face,
  Though we were changed and changing;
If, *then*, some natural shadows spread
  Our inward prospect over,
The soul's deep valley was not slow
  Its brightness to recover.

Eternal blessings on the Muse,
    And her divine employment !
The blameless Muse, who trains her Sons
    For hope and calm enjoyment ;
Albeit sickness, lingering yet,
    Has o'er their pillow brooded ;
And Care waylays their steps—a Sprite
    Not easily eluded.

For thee, O SCOTT ! compelled to change
    Green Eildon Hill and Cheviot
For warm Vesuvio's vine-clad slopes ;
    And leave thy Tweed and Teviot
For mild Sorrento's breezy waves ;
    May classic Fancy, linking
With native Fancy her fresh aid,
    Preserve thy heart from sinking !

O ! while they minister to thee,
    Each vying with the other,
May Health return to mellow Age
    With Strength her venturous brother ;
And Tiber, and each brook and rill
    'Renowned in song and story,
With unimagined beauty shine,
    Nor lose one ray of glory !

For Thou, upon a hundred streams,
    By tales of love and sorrow,
Of faithful love, undaunted truth,
    Hast shed the power of Yarrow ;

And streams unknown, hills yet unseen,
　Wherever they invite Thee,
At parent Nature's grateful call,
　With gladness must requite Thee.

A gracious welcome shall be thine,
　Such looks of love and honour
As thy own Yarrow gave to me
　When first I gazed upon her;
Beheld what I had feared to see,
　Unwilling to surrender
Dreams treasured up from early days,
　The holy and the tender.

And what, for this frail world, were all
　That mortals do or suffer,
Did no responsive harp, no pen,
　Memorial tribute offer?
Yea, what were mighty Nature's self?
　Her features, could they win us,
Unhelped by that poetic voice
　That hourly speaks within us?

Nor deem that localised Romance
　Plays false with our affections;
Unsanctifies our tears—made sport
　For fanciful dejections:
Oh, no! the visions of the past
　Sustain the heart in feeling
Life as she is—our changeful Life,
　With friends and kindred dealing.

Bear witness, Ye, whose thoughts that day
  In Yarrow's groves were centred;
Who through the silent portal arch
  Of mouldering Newark enter'd;
And clomb the winding stair that once
  Too timidly was mounted
By the 'last Minstrel' (not the last!)
  Ere he his Tale recounted.

Flow on for ever, Yarrow Stream!
  Fulfil thy pensive duty,
Well pleased that future Bards should chant
  For simple hearts thy beauty;
To dream-light dear while yet unseen,
  Dear to the common sunshine,
And dearer still, as now I feel,
  To memory's shadowy moonshine!

ON THE DEPARTURE OF SIR
WALTER SCOTT

FROM ABBOTSFORD FOR NAPLES

A TROUBLE, not of clouds, or weeping rain,
    Nor of the setting sun's pathetic light
Engendered, hangs o'er Eildon's triple height:
Spirits of Power, assembled there, complain
For kindred Power departing from their sight;
While Tweed, best pleased in chanting a blithe strain,
Saddens his voice again, and yet again.
Lift up your hearts, ye Mourners! for the might
Of the whole world's good wishes with him goes;
Blessings and prayers in nobler retinue

Than sceptred king or laurelled conqueror knows,
Follow this wondrous Potentate.   Be true,
Ye winds of ocean, and the midland sea,
Wafting your Charge to soft Parthenope!

THE TROSSACHS

THERE'S not a nook within this solemn Pass,
    But were an apt confessional for One
Taught by his summer spent, his autumn gone,
That Life is but a tale of morning grass
Withered at eve.   From scenes of art which chase
That thought away, turn, and with watchful eyes
Feed it 'mid Nature's old felicities,
Rocks, rivers, and smooth lakes more clear than glass
Untouched, unbreathed upon.   Thrice happy quest,
If from a golden perch of aspen spray
(October's workmanship to rival May)
The pensive warbler of the ruddy breast
That moral sweeten by a heaven-taught lay,
Lulling the year, with all its cares, to rest!

HIGHLAND HUT

SEE what gay wild flowers deck this earth-built Cot
    Whose smoke, forth-issuing whence and how it
      may,
Shines in the greeting of the sun's first ray
Like wreaths of vapour without stain or blot.
The limpid mountain rill avoids it not;
And why shouldst thou?—If rightly trained and bred
Humanity is humble, finds no spot
Which her Heaven-guided feet refuse to tread.

The walls are cracked, sunk is the flowery roof,
Undressed the pathway leading to the door;
But love, as Nature loves, the lonely Poor;
Search, for their worth, some gentle heart wrong-proof,
Meek, patient, kind, and, were its trials fewer,
Belike less happy.—Stand no more aloof!

EVENING VOLUNTARIES

NOT in the lucid intervals of life
    That come but as a curse to party strife;
Not in some hour when Pleasure with a sigh
Of languor puts his rosy garland by;
Not in the breathing-times of that poor slave
Who daily piles up wealth in Mammon's cave—
Is Nature felt, or can be; nor do words,
Which practised talent readily affords,
Prove that her hand has touched responsive chords;
Nor has her gentle beauty power to move
With genuine rapture and with fervent love
The soul of Genius, if he dare to take
Life's rule from passion craved for passion's sake;
Untaught that meekness is the cherished bent
Of all the truly great and all the innocent.

    But who *is* innocent?   By grace divine,
Not otherwise, O Nature! we are thine,
Through good and evil thine, in just degree
Of rational and manly sympathy.
To all that Earth from pensive hearts is stealing,
And Heaven is now to gladdened eyes revealing,
Add every charm the Universe can show
Through every change its aspects undergo—

Care may be respited, but not repealed;
No perfect cure grows on that bounded field.
Vain is the pleasure, a false calm the peace,
If He, through whom alone our conflicts
    cease,
Our virtuous hopes without relapse advance,
Come not to speed the Soul's deliverance;
To the distempered Intellect refuse
His gracious help, or give what we abuse.

1834.

COMPOSED UPON AN EVENING OF EX-
    TRAORDINARY SPLENDOUR AND
    BEAUTY

HAD this effulgence disappeared
    With flying haste, I might have sent,
Among the speechless clouds, a look
Of blank astonishment;
But 'tis endued with power to stay,
And sanctify one closing day,
That frail Mortality may see—
What is?—ah no, but what *can* be!
Time was when field and watery cove
With modulated echoes rang,
While choirs of fervent Angels sang
Their vespers in the grove;
Or, crowning, star-like, each some sovereign
    height,
Warbled, for heaven above and earth below,
Strains suitable to both.—Such holy rite,
Methinks, if audibly repeated now

From hill or valley, could not move
Sublimer transport, purer love,
Than doth this silent spectacle—the gleam—
The shadow—and the peace supreme!

No sound is uttered,—but a deep
And solemn harmony pervades
The hollow vale from steep to steep,
And penetrates the glades.
Far-distant images draw nigh,
Called forth by wondrous potency
Of beamy radiance, that imbues
Whate'er it strikes with gem-like hues!
In vision exquisitely clear,
Herds range along the mountain side;
And glistening antlers are descried;
And gilded flocks appear.
Thine is the tranquil hour, purpureal Eve!
But long as god-like wish, or hope divine,
Informs my spirit, ne'er can I believe
That this magnificence is wholly thine!
—From worlds not quickened by the sun
A portion of the gift is won;
An intermingling of Heaven's pomp is spread
On ground which British shepherds tread!

And, if there be whom broken ties
Afflict, or injuries assail,
Yon hazy ridges to their eyes
Present a glorious scale,
Climbing suffused with sunny air,
To stop—no record hath told where!

And tempting Fancy to ascend,
And with immortal Spirits blend!
—Wings at my shoulders seem to play;
But, rooted here, I stand and gaze
On those bright steps that heavenward raise
Their practicable way.
Come forth, ye drooping old men, look abroad,
And see to what fair countries ye are bound!
And if some traveller, weary of his road,
Hath slept since noon-tide on the grassy
    ground,
Ye Genii! to his covert speed;
And wake him with such gentle heed
As may attune his soul to meet the dower
Bestowed on this transcendent hour!

Such hues from their celestial Urn
Were wont to stream before mine eye,
Where'er it wandered in the morn
Of blissful infancy.
This glimpse of glory, why renewed?
Nay, rather speak with gratitude;
For, if a vestige of those gleams
Survived, 'twas only in my dreams.
Dread Power! whom peace and calmness
    serve
No less than Nature's threatening voice,
If aught unworthy be my choice,
From THEE if I would swerve;
Oh, let thy grace remind me of the light
Full early lost, and fruitlessly deplored;
Which, at this moment, on my waking sight
Appears to shine, by miracle restored;

My soul, though yet confined to earth,
Rejoices in a second birth!
—'Tis past, the visionary splendour fades;
And night approaches with her shades.
      1818.

WRITTEN ON A BLANK LEAF OF MACPHERSON'S 'OSSIAN'

OFT have I caught, upon a fitful breeze,
      Fragments of far-off melodies,
With ear not coveting the whole,
A part so charmed the pensive soul:
While a dark storm before my sight
Was yielding, on a mountain height
Loose vapours have I watched, that won
Prismatic colours from the sun;
Nor felt a wish that heaven would show
The image of its perfect bow.
What need, then, of these finished Strains?
Away with counterfeit Remains!
An abbey in its lone recess,
A temple of the wilderness,
Wrecks though they be, announce with feeling
The majesty of honest dealing.
Spirit of Ossian! if imbound
In language thou may'st yet be found,
If aught (intrusted to the pen
Or floating on the tongues of men,
Albeit shattered and impaired)
Subsist thy dignity to guard,
In concert with memorial claim
Of old grey stone, and high-born name

That cleaves to rock or pillared cave
Where moans the blast, or beats the wave,
Let Truth, stern arbitress of all,
Interpret that Original,
And for presumptuous wrongs atone;—
Authentic words be given, or none!

Time is not blind;—yet He, who spares
Pyramid pointing to the stars,
Hath preyed with ruthless appetite
On all that marked the primal flight
Of the poetic ecstasy
Into the land of mystery.
No tongue is able to rehearse
One measure, Orpheus! of thy verse;
Musæus, stationed with his lyre
Supreme among the Elysian quire,
Is, for the dwellers upon earth,
Mute as a lark ere morning's birth.
Why grieve for these, though past away
The music, and extinct the lay?
When thousands, by severer doom,
Full early to the silent tomb
Have sunk, at Nature's call; or strayed
From hope and promise, self-betrayed;
The garland withering on their brows;
Stung with remorse for broken vows;
Frantic—else how might they rejoice?
And friendless, by their own sad choice!

Hail, Bards of mightier grasp! on you
I chiefly call, the chosen Few,
Who cast not off the acknowledged guide,
Who faltered not, nor turned aside;

Whose lofty genius could survive
Privation, under sorrow thrive;
In whom the fiery Muse revered
The symbol of a snow-white beard,
Bedewed with meditative tears
Dropped from the lenient cloud of years.

Brothers in soul! though distant times
Produced you nursed in various climes,
Ye, when the orb of life had waned,
A plenitude of love retained:
Hence, while in you each sad regret
By corresponding hope was met,
Ye lingered among human kind,
Sweet voices for the passing wind;
Departing sunbeams, loth to stop,
Though smiling on the last hill top!
Such to the tender-hearted maid
Even ere her joys begin to fade;
Such, haply, to the rugged chief
By fortune crushed, or tamed by grief;
Appears, on Morven's lonely shore,
Dim-gleaming through imperfect lore,
The Son of Fingal; such was blind
Mæonides of ampler mind;
Such Milton, to the fountain head
Of glory by Urania led!
1824.

MOST sweet it is with unuplifted eyes
To pace the ground, if path be there or none,
While a fair region round the traveller lies
Which he forbears again to look upon;

Pleased rather with some soft ideal scene,
The work of Fancy, or some happy tone
Of meditation, slipping in between
The beauty coming and the beauty gone.
If Thought and Love desert us, from that day
Let us break off all commerce with the Muse:
With Thought and Love companions of our way,
Whate'er the senses take or may refuse,
The Mind's internal heaven shall shed her dews
Of inspiration on the humblest lay.

POEMS OF SENTIMENT AND
REFLECTION

EXPOSTULATION AND REPLY

'WHY, William, on that old grey stone,
   Thus for the length of half a day,
Why, William, sit you thus alone,
And dream your time away?

'Where are your books?—that light bequeathed
To Beings else forlorn and blind!
Up! up! and drink the spirit breathed
From dead men to their kind.

'You look round on your Mother Earth,
As if she for no purpose bore you;
As if you were her first-born birth,
And none had lived before you!'

One morning thus, by Esthwaite lake,
When life was sweet, I knew not why,
To me my good friend Matthew spake,
And thus I made reply:

'The eye—it cannot choose but see:
We cannot bid the ear be still;
Our bodies feel, where'er they be,
Against or with our will.

'Nor less I deem that there are Powers
Which of themselves our minds impress;
That we can feed this mind of ours
In a wise passiveness.

'Think you, 'mid all this mighty sum
Of things for ever speaking,
That nothing of itself will come,
But we must still be seeking!

'Then ask not wherefore, here, alone,
Conversing as I may,
I sit upon this old grey stone,
And dream my time away.'

    1798.

THE TABLES TURNED

AN EVENING SCENE ON THE SAME SUBJECT

UP! up! my Friend, and quit your books;
   Or surely you'll grow double:
Up! up! my Friend, and clear your looks;
Why all this toil and trouble?

The sun, above the mountain's head,
A freshening lustre mellow
Through all the long green fields has spread,
His first sweet evening yellow.

Books! 'tis a dull and endless strife:
Come, hear the woodland linnet,
How sweet his music! on my life,
There's more of wisdom in it.

And hark! how blithe the throstle sings!
He, too, is no mean preacher:
Come forth into the light of things,
Let Nature be your teacher.

She has a world of ready wealth,
Our minds and hearts to bless—
Spontaneous wisdom breathed by health,
Truth breathed by cheerfulness.

One impulse from a vernal wood
May teach you more of man,
Of moral evil and of good,
Than all the sages can.

Sweet is the lore which Nature brings;
Our meddling intellect
Mis-shapes the beauteous forms of things:
We murder to dissect.

Enough of Science and of Art;
Close up those barren leaves;
Come forth, and bring with you a heart
That watches and receives.
1798.

LINES WRITTEN IN EARLY SPRING

I HEARD a thousand blended notes,
　　While in a grove I sate reclined,
In that sweet mood when pleasant thoughts
Bring sad thoughts to the mind.

To her fair works did Nature link
The human soul that through me ran ;
And much it grieved my heart to think
What man has made of man.

Through primrose tufts, in that green bower,
The periwinkle trailed its wreaths ;
And 'tis my faith that every flower
Enjoys the air it breathes.

The birds around me hopped and played,
Their thoughts I cannot measure :—
But the least motion which they made,
It seemed a thrill of pleasure.

The budding twigs spread out their fan,
To catch the breezy air ;
And I must think, do all I can,
That there was pleasure there.

If this belief from heaven be sent,
If such be Nature's holy plan,
Have I not reason to lament
What man has made of man ?
　　1798.

TO MY SISTER

IT is the first mild day of March:
  Each minute sweeter than before;
The redbreast sings from the tall larch
That stands beside our door.

There is a blessing in the air,
Which seems a sense of joy to yield
To the bare trees, and mountains bare,
And grass in the green field.

My sister! ('tis a wish of mine)
Now that our morning meal is done,
Make haste, your morning task resign;
Come forth and feel the sun.

Edward will come with you;—and, pray,
Put on with speed your woodland dress;
And bring no book: for this one day
We'll give to idleness.

No joyless forms shall regulate
Our living calendar:
We from to-day, my Friend, will date
The opening of the year.

Love, now a universal birth,
From heart to heart is stealing,
From earth to man, from man to earth:
—It is the hour of feeling.

One moment now may give us more
Than years of toiling reason :
Our minds shall drink at every pore
The spirit of the season.

Some silent laws our hearts will make,
Which they shall long obey :
We for the year to come may take
Our temper from to-day.

And from the blesséd power that rolls
About, below, above,
We'll frame the measure of our souls :
They shall be tuned to love.

Then come, my Sister ! come, I pray,
With speed put on your woodland dress ;
And bring no book : for this one day
We'll give to idleness.

   1798.

SIMON LEE, THE OLD HUNTSMAN

WITH AN INCIDENT IN WHICH HE WAS CONCERNED

IN the sweet shire of Cardigan,
  Not far from pleasant Ivor Hall,
An old Man dwells, a little man,—
'Tis said he once was tall.
Full five-and-thirty years he lived
A running huntsman merry ;
And still the centre of his cheek
Is red as a ripe cherry.

No man like him the horn could sound,
And hill and valley rang with glee
When Echo bandied, round and round,
The halloo of Simon Lee.
In those proud days, he little cared
For husbandry or tillage ;
To blither tasks did Simon rouse
The sleepers of the village.

He all the country could outrun,
Could leave both man and horse behind ;
And often, ere the chase was done,
He reeled, and was stone-blind.
And still there's something in the world
At which his heart rejoices ;
For when the chiming hounds are out,
He dearly loves their voices !

But, oh the heavy change !—bereft
Of health, strength, friends, and kindred, see !
Old Simon to the world is left
In liveried poverty.
His Master's dead,—and no one now
Dwells in the Hall of Ivor ;
Men, dogs, and horses, all are dead ;
He is the sole survivor.

And he is lean and he is sick ;
His body, dwindled and awry,
Rests upon ankles swollen and thick ;
His legs are thin and dry.

One prop he has, and only one:
His wife, an aged woman,
Lives with him, near the waterfall:
Upon the village Common.

Beside their moss-grown hut of clay,
Not twenty paces from the door,
A scrap of land they have, but they
Are poorest of the poor.
This scrap of land he from the heath
Enclosed when he was stronger;
But what to them avails the land
Which he can till no longer?

Oft, working by her Husband's side,
Ruth does what Simon cannot do;
For she, with scanty cause for pride,
Is stouter of the two.
And, though you with your utmost skill
From labour could not wean them,
'Tis little, very little—all
That they can do between them.

Few months of life has he in store,
As he to you will tell,
For still, the more he works, the more
Do his weak ankles swell.
My gentle Reader, I perceive
How patiently you've waited,
And now I fear that you expect
Some tale will be related.

O Reader! had you in your mind
Such stores as silent thought can bring,
O gentle Reader! you would find
A tale in everything.
What more I have to say is short,
And you must kindly take it:
It is no tale; but, should you think,
Perhaps a tale you'll make it.

One summer day I chanced to see
This old Man doing all he could
To unearth the root of an old tree,
A stump of rotten wood.
The mattock tottered in his hand;
So vain was his endeavour,
That at the root of the old tree
He might have worked for ever.

'You're overtasked, good Simon Lee,
Give me your tool,' to him I said;
And at the word right gladly he
Received my proffered aid.
I struck, and with a single blow
The tangled root I severed,
At which the poor old Man so long
And vainly had endeavoured.

The tears into his eyes were brought,
And thanks and praises seemed to run
So fast out of his heart, I thought
They never would have done

—I've heard of hearts unkind, kind deeds
With coldness still returning ;
Alas ! the gratitude of men
Hath oftener left me mourning.
1798.

A POET'S EPITAPH

ART thou a Statist in the van
    Of public conflicts trained and bred ?
—First learn to love one living man ;
Then may'st thou think upon the dead.

A Lawyer art thou ?—draw not nigh !
Go, carry to some fitter place
The keenness of that practised eye,
The hardness of that sallow face.

Art thou a Man of purple cheer ?
A rosy Man, right plump to see ?
Approach ; yet, Doctor, not too near,
This grave no cushion is for thee.

Or art thou one of gallant pride,
A Soldier and no man of chaff ?
Welcome !—but lay thy sword aside,
And lean upon a peasant's staff.

Physician are thou ? one all eyes,
Philosopher ! a fingering slave,
One that would peep and botanise
Upon his mother's grave ?

Wrapt closely in thy sensual fleece,
O turn aside,—and take, I pray,
That he below may rest in peace,
Thy ever-dwindling soul, away!

A Moralist perchance appears;
Led, Heaven knows how! to this poor sod:
And he has neither eyes nor ears;
Himself his world, and his own God;

One to whose smooth-rubbed soul can cling
Nor form, nor feeling, great or small;
A reasoning, self-sufficing thing,
An intellectual All-in-all!

Shut close the door; press down the latch;
Sleep in thy intellectual crust;
Nor lose ten tickings of thy watch
Near this unprofitable dust.

But who is He, with modest looks,
And clad in homely russet brown?
He murmurs near the running brooks
A music sweeter than their own.

He is retired as noontide dew,
Or fountain in a noon-day grove;
And you must love him, ere to you
He will seem worthy of your love.

The outward shows of sky and earth,
Of hill and valley, he has viewed;
And impulses of deeper birth
Have come to him in solitude.

In common things that round us lie
Some random truths he can impart,—
The harvest of a quiet eye
That broods and sleeps on his own heart.

But he is weak; both Man and Boy,
Hath been an idler in the land;
Contented if he might enjoy
The things which others understand.

—Come hither in thy hour of strength;
Come, weak as is a breaking wave!
Here stretch thy body at full length;
Or build thy house upon this grave.
    1799.

MATTHEW

In the school of —— is a tablet, on which are inscribed, in gilt
letters, the names of the several persons who have been school-
masters there since the foundation of the school, with the time
at which they entered upon and quitted their office. Opposite
to one of those names the author wrote the following lines.

IF Nature, for a favourite child,
    In thee hath tempered so her clay,
That every hour thy heart runs wild,
Yet never once doth go astray,

Read o'er these lines; and then review
This tablet, that thus humbly rears
In such diversity of hue
Its history of two hundred years.

—When through this little wreck of fame,
Cipher and syllable! thine eye
Has travelled down to Matthew's name,
Pause with no common sympathy.

And, if a sleeping tear should wake,
Then be it neither checked nor stayed:
For Matthew a request I make
Which for himself he had not made.

Poor Matthew, all his frolics o'er,
Is silent as a standing pool;
Far from the chimney's merry roar,
And murmur of the village school.

The sighs which Matthew heaved were sighs
Of one tired out with fun and madness;
The tears which came to Matthew's eyes
Were tears of light, the dew of gladness.

Yet, sometimes, when the secret cup
Of still and serious thought went round,
It seemed as if he drank it up—
He felt with spirit so profound.

—Thou soul of God's best earthly mould!
Thou happy Soul! and can it be
That these two words of glittering gold
Are all that must remain of thee?

1799.

THE TWO APRIL MORNINGS

WE walked along, while bright and red
    Uprose the morning sun;
And Matthew stopped, he looked, and said,
'The will of God be done!'

A village schoolmaster was he,
With hair of glittering grey;
As blithe a man as you could see
On a spring holiday.

And on that morning, through the grass,
And by the steaming rills,
We travelled merrily, to pass
A day among the hills.

'Our work,' said I, 'was well begun:
Then, from thy breast what thought,
Beneath so beautiful a sun,
So sad a sigh has brought?'

A second time did Matthew stop
And fixing still his eye
Upon the eastern mountain-top,
To me he made reply:

'Yon cloud with that long purple cleft
Brings fresh into my mind
A day like this which I have left
Full thirty years behind.

'And just above yon slope of corn
Such colours, and no other,
Were in the sky, that April morn,
Of this the very brother.

'With rod and line I sued the sport
Which that sweet season gave,
And, to the churchyard come, stopped short
Beside my daughter's grave,

'Nine summers had she scarcely seen,
The pride of all the vale;
And then she sang;—she would have been
A very nightingale.

'Six feet in earth my Emma lay;
And yet I loved her more,
For so it seemed, than till that day
I e'er had loved before.

'And, turning from her grave, I met,
Beside the churchyard yew,
A blooming Girl, whose hair was wet
With points of morning dew.

'A basket on her head she bare;
Her brow was smooth and white:
To see a child so very fair,
It was a pure delight!

'No fountain from its rocky cave
E'er tripped with foot so free;
She seemed as happy as a wave
That dances on the sea.

'There came from me a sigh of pain
Which I could ill confine;
I looked at her, and looked again:
And did not wish her mine!'

Matthew is in his grave, yet now,
Methinks, I see him stand,
As at that moment, with a bough
Of wilding in his hand.

1799.

THE FOUNTAIN

A CONVERSATION

WE talked with open heart, and tongue
    Affectionate and true,
A pair of friends, though I was young,
And Matthew seventy-two.

We lay beneath a spreading oak,
Beside a mossy seat;
And from the turf a fountain broke,
And gurgled at our feet.

'Now, Matthew!' said I, 'let us match
This water's pleasant tune
With some old border-song, or catch
That suits a summer's noon;

'Or of the church-clock and the chimes
Sing here beneath the shade,
That half-mad thing of witty rhymes
Which you last April made!'

In silence Matthew lay, and eyed
The spring beneath the tree;
And thus the dear old Man replied,
The grey-haired Man of glee:

'No check, no stay, this streamlet fears;
How merrily it goes!
'Twill murmur on a thousand years,
And flow as now it flows.

'And here, on this delightful day,
I cannot choose but think
How oft, a vigorous man, I lay
Beside this fountain's brink.

'My eyes are dim with childish tears,
My heart is idly stirred,
For the same sound is in my ears
Which in those days I heard.

'Thus fares it still in our decay:
And yet the wiser mind
Mourns less for what age takes away
Than what it leaves behind.

'The blackbird amid leafy trees,
The lark above the hill,
Let loose their carols when they please,
Are quiet when they will.

'With Nature never do *they* wage
A foolish strife; they see
A happy youth, and their old age
Is beautiful and free:

'But we are pressed by heavy laws;
And often, glad no more,
We wear a face of joy, because
We have been glad of yore.

'If there be one who need bemoan
His kindred laid in earth,
The household hearts that were his own;
It is the man of mirth.

'My days, my Friend, are almost gone,
My life has been approved,
And many love me; but by none
Am I enough beloved.'

'Now both himself and me he wrongs,
The man who thus complains!
I live and sing my idle songs
Upon these happy plains;

'And, Matthew, for thy children dead
I'll be a son to thee!'
At this he grasped my hand, and said,
'Alas! that cannot be.'

We rose up from the fountain-side;
And down the smooth descent
Of the green sheep-track did we glide;
And through the wood we went;

And, ere we came to Leonard's rock,
He sang those witty rhymes
About the crazy old church-clock,
And the bewildered chimes.

  1799.

FIDELITY

A BARKING sound the Shepherd hears,
  A cry as of a dog or fox;
He halts—and searches with his eyes
Among the scattered rocks:
And now at distance can discern
A stirring in a brake of fern;
And instantly a dog is seen,
Glancing through that covert green.

The Dog is not of mountain breed;
Its motions, too, are wild and shy;
With something, as the Shepherd thinks,
Unusual in its cry:
Nor is there any one in sight
All round, in hollow or on height;
Nor shout, nor whistle strikes his ear;
What is the creature doing here?

It was a cove, a huge recess,
That keeps, till June, December's snow;
A lofty precipice in front,
A silent tarn below!
Far in the bosom of Helvellyn,
Remote from public road or dwelling,
Pathway, or cultivated land;
From trace of human foot or hand.

There sometimes doth a leaping fish
Send through the tarn a lonely cheer;
The crags repeat the raven's croak,
In symphony austere;

Thither the rainbow comes—the cloud—
And mists that spread the flying shroud;
And sunbeams; and the sounding blast,
That, if it could, would hurry past;
But that enormous barrier holds it fast.

Not free from boding thoughts, a while
The Shepherd stood; then makes his way
O'er rocks and stones, following the Dog
As quickly as he may;
Nor far had gone before he found
A human skeleton on the ground;
The appalled Discoverer with a sigh
Looks round to learn the history.

From those abrupt and perilous rocks
The Man had fallen, that place of fear!
At length upon the Shepherd's mind
It breaks, and all is clear:
He instantly recalled the name,
And who he was, and whence he came;
Remembered, too, the very day
On which the Traveller passed this way.

But hear a wonder, for whose sake
This lamentable tale I tell!
A lasting monument of words
This wonder merits well.
The Dog, which still was hovering nigh,
Repeating the same timid cry,
This Dog, had been through three months' space
A dweller in that savage place.

Yes, proof was plain that, since the day
When this ill-fated Traveller died,
The Dog had watched about the spot,
Or by his master's side :
How nourished here through such long time
He knows, who gave that love sublime ;
And gave that strength of feeling, great
Above all human estimate !
   1805.

ODE TO DUTY

' Jam non consilio bonus, sed more eò perductus, ut non tantum
rectè facere possim, sed nisi rectè facere non possim.'

STERN Daughter of the Voice of God !
  O Duty ! if that name thou love,
Who art a light to guide, a rod
To check the erring, and reprove ;
Thou, who art victory and law
When empty terrors overawe ;
From vain temptations dost set free ;
And calm'st the weary strife of frail humanity !

There are who ask not if thine eye
Be on them ; who, in love and truth,
Where no misgiving is, rely
Upon the genial sense of youth :
Glad Hearts ! without reproach or blot ;
Who do thy work, and know it not :
Oh ! if through confidence misplaced
They fail, thy saving arms, dread Power ! around them
    cast.

Serene will be our days and bright,
And happy will our nature be,
When love is an unerring light,
And joy its own security.
And they a blissful course may hold
Even now, who, not unwisely bold,
Live in the spirit of this creed;
Yet seek thy firm support, according to their need.

I, loving freedom, and untried;
No sport of every random gust,
Yet being to myself a guide,
Too blindly have reposed my trust:
And oft, when in my heart was heard
Thy timely mandate, I deferred
The task, in smoother walks to stray;
But thee I now would serve more strictly, if I may.

Through no disturbance of my soul,
Or strong compunction in me wrought,
I supplicate for thy control;
But in the quietness of thought:
Me this unchartered freedom tires;
I feel the weight of chance-desires:
My hopes no more must change their name,
I long for a repose that ever is the same.

Stern Lawgiver! yet thou dost wear
The Godhead's most benignant grace;
Nor know we anything so fair
As is the smile upon thy face:

Flowers laugh before thee on their beds;
And fragrance in thy footing treads;
Thou dost preserve the stars from wrong;
And the most ancient heavens, through thee, are
    fresh and strong.

To humbler functions, awful Power!
I call thee: I myself commend
Unto thy guidance from this hour;
Oh, let my weakness have an end!
Give unto me, made lowly wise,
The spirit of self-sacrifice;
The confidence of reason give;
And in the light of truth thy Bondman let me live!
    1805.

CHARACTER OF THE HAPPY WARRIOR

WHO is the happy Warrior? Who is he
    That every man in arms should wish to be?
—It is the generous Spirit, who, when brought
Among the tasks of real life, hath wrought
Upon the plan that pleased his boyish thought:
Whose high endeavours are an inward light
That makes the path before him always bright:
Who, with a natural instinct to discern
What knowledge can perform, is diligent to learn;
Abides by this resolve, and stops not there,
But makes his moral being his prime care;
Who, doomed to go in company with Pain,
And Fear, and Bloodshed, miserable train!
Turns his necessity to glorious gain;

In face of these doth exercise a power
Which is our human nature's highest dower;
Controls them and subdues, transmutes, bereaves
Of their bad influence, and their good receives:
By objects, which might force the soul to abate
Her feeling, rendered more compassionate;
Is placable—because occasions rise
So often that demand such sacrifice;
More skilful in self-knowledge, even more pure,
As tempted more; more able to endure,
As more exposed to suffering and distress;
Thence, also, more alive to tenderness.
—'Tis he whose law is reason; who depends
Upon that law as on the best of friends;
Whence, in a state where men are tempted still
To evil for a guard against worse ill,
And what in quality or act is best
Doth seldom on a right foundation rest,
He labours good on good to fix, and owes
To virtue every triumph that he knows:
—Who, if he rise to station of command,
Rises by open means; and there will stand
On honourable terms, or else retire,
And in himself possess his own desire;
Who comprehends his trust, and to the same
Keeps faithful with a singleness of aim;
And therefore does not stoop, nor lie in wait
For wealth, or honours, or for worldly state;
Whom they must follow; on whose head must fall,
Like showers of manna, if they come at all:
Whose powers shed round him in the common
        strife,
Or mild concerns of ordinary life,

A constant influence, a peculiar grace ;
But who, if he be called upon to face
Some awful moment to which Heaven has joined
Great issues, good or bad for human kind,
Is happy as a Lover ; and attired
With sudden brightness, like a Man inspired ;
And, through the heat of conflict, keeps the law
In calmness made, and sees what he foresaw ;
Or if an unexpected call succeed,
Come when it will, is equal to the need :
—He who, though thus endued as with a sense
And faculty for storm and turbulence,
Is yet a Soul whose master-bias leans
To homefelt pleasures and to gentle scenes ;
Sweet images ! which, wheresoe'er he be,
Are at his heart ; and such fidelity
It is his darling passion to approve ;
More brave for this, that he hath much to love :—
'Tis, finally, the Man, who, lifted high,
Conspicuous object in a Nation's eye,
Or left unthought-of in obscurity,—
Who, with a toward or untoward lot,
Prosperous or adverse, to his wish or not—
Plays, in the many games of life, that one
Where what he most doth value must be won :
Whom neither shape of danger can dismay,
Nor thought of tender happiness betray ;
Who, not content that former worth stand fast,
Looks forward, persevering to the last,
From well to better, daily self-surpast :
Who, whether praise of him must walk the
    earth
For ever, and to noble deeds give birth,

Or he must fall, to sleep without his fame,
And leave a dead unprofitable name—
Finds comfort in himself and in his cause;
And, while the mortal mist is gathering, draws
His breath in confidence of Heaven's applause:
This is the happy Warrior; this is He
That every Man in arms should wish to be.

    1806.

ODE TO LYCORIS

ENOUGH of climbing toil!—Ambition treads
    Here, as 'mid busier scenes, ground steep and
    rough,
Or slippery even to peril! and each step
As we for most uncertain recompense
Mount toward the empire of the fickle clouds,
Each weary step, dwarfing the world below,
Induces, for its old familiar sights,
Unacceptable feelings of contempt,
With wonder mixed—that Man could e'er be tied,
In anxious bondage, to such nice array
And formal fellowship of petty things!
—Oh! 'tis the *heart* that magnifies this life,
Making a truth and beauty of her own;
And moss-grown alleys, circumscribing shades,
And gurgling rills, assist her in the work
More efficaciously than realms outspread,
As in a map, before the adventurer's gaze—
Ocean and Earth contending for regard.

    The umbrageous woods are left—how far beneath!
But lo! where darkness seems to guard the mouth

Of yon wild cave, whose jaggéd brows are fringed
With flaccid threads of ivy, in the still
And sultry air, depending motionless
Yet cool the space within, and not uncheered
(As whoso enters shall ere long perceive)
By stealthy influx of the timid day
Mingling with night, such twilight to compose
As Numa loved ; when, in the Egerian grot,
From the sage Nymph appearing at his wish,
He gained whate'er a regal mind might ask,
Or need, of counsel breathed through lips divine.

Long as the heat shall rage, let that dim cave
Protect us, there deciphering as we may
Diluvian records ; or the sighs of Earth
Interpreting ; or counting for old Time
His minutes, by reiterated drops,
Audible tears, from some invisible source
That deepens upon fancy—more and more
Drawn toward the centre whence those sighs creep forth
To awe the lightness of humanity.
Or, shutting up thyself within thyself,
There let me see thee sink into a mood
Of gentler thought, protracted till thine eye
Be calm as water when the winds are gone,
And no one can tell whither.   Dearest friend !
We two have known such happy hours together
That, were power granted to replace them (fetched
From out the pensive shadows where they lie)
In the first warmth of their original sunshine,
Loth should I be to use it : passing sweet
Are the domains of tender memory !

1817.

PATIENCE

IF this great world of joy and pain
    Revolve in one sure track;
If freedom, set, will rise again,
    And virtue, flown, come back;
Woe to the purblind crew who fill
    The heart with each day's care;
Nor gain, from past or future, skill
    To bear, and to forbear!

    1833.

TO MAY

THOUGH many suns have risen and set
    Since thou, blythe May, wert born,
And Bards, who hailed thee, may forget
    Thy gifts, thy beauty scorn:
There are who to a birthday strain
    Confine not harp and voice,
But evermore throughout thy reign
    Are grateful and rejoice!

Delicious odours! music sweet,
    Too sweet to pass away!
Oh for a deathless song to meet
    The soul's desire—a lay
That, when a thousand years are told,
    Should praise thee, genial power!
Through summer heat, autumnal cold,
    And winter's dreariest hour.

Earth, Sea, thy presence feel—nor less,
   If yon ethereal blue
With its soft smile the truth express
   The Heavens have felt it too.
The inmost heart of man if glad
   Partakes a livelier cheer;
And eyes that cannot but be sad
   Let fall a brightened tear.

Since thy return, through days and weeks
   Of hope that grew by stealth,
How many wan and faded cheeks
   Have kindled into health!
The Old, by thee revived, have said,
   'Another year is ours:'
And wayworn Wanderers, poorly fed,
   Have smiled upon thy flowers.

Who tripping lisps a merry song
   Amid his playful peers?
The tender Infant who was long
   A prisoner of fond fears;
But now, when every sharp-edged blast
   Is quiet in its sheath
His Mother leaves him free to taste
   Earth's sweetness in thy breath.

Thy help is with the weed that creeps
   Along the humblest ground;
No cliff so bare but on its steeps
   Thy favours may be found;

But most on some peculiar nook
   That our own hands have drest,
Thou and thy train are proud to look,
   And seem to love it best.

And yet how pleased we wander forth
   When May is whispering, 'Come!
Choose from the bowers of virgin earth
   The happiest for your home ;
Heaven's bounteous love through me is spread
   From sunshine, clouds, winds, waves,
Drops on the mouldering turret's head,
   And on your turf-clad graves !'

Such greeting heard, away with sighs
   For lilies that must fade,
Or 'the rathe primrose as it dies
   Forsaken' in the shade !
Vernal fruitions and desires
   Are linked in endless chase :
While, as one kindly growth retires,
   Another takes its place.

And what if thou, sweet May, hast known
   Mishap by worm and blight ;
If expectations newly blown
   Have perished in thy sight ;
If loves and joys, while up they sprung,
   Were caught as in a snare ;
Such is the lot of all the young,
   However bright and fair.

Lo! Streams that April could not check
  Are patient of thy rule;
Gurgling in foamy water-break,
  Loitering in glassy pool:
By thee, thee only, could be sent
  Such gentle mists as glide,
Curling with unconfirmed intent,
  On that green mountain's side.

How delicate the leafy veil
  Through which yon house of God
Gleams 'mid the peace of this deep dale
  By few but shepherds trod!
And lowly huts, near beaten ways,
  No sooner stand attired
In thy fresh wreaths, than they for praise
  Peep forth, and are admired.

Season of fancy and of hope,
  Permit not for one hour
A blossom from thy crown to drop,
  Nor add to it a flower!
Keep, lovely May, as if by touch
  Of self-restraining art,
This modest charm of not too much,
  Part seen, imagined part!
    1826-1834.

POEMS REFERRING TO THE
PERIOD OF OLD AGE

THE OLD CUMBERLAND BEGGAR

The class of Beggars to which the old man here described belongs will probably soon be extinct. It consisted of poor and mostly old and infirm persons, who confined themselves to a stated round in their neighbourhood, and had certain fixed days, on which, at different houses, they regularly received alms, sometimes in money, but mostly in provisions.

I SAW an aged Beggar in my walk ;
And he was seated, by the highway side,
On a low structure of rude masonry
Built at the foot of a huge hill, that they
Who lead their horses down the steep rough road
May thence remount at ease.   The aged man
Had placed his staff across the broad smooth
    stone
That overlays the pile ; and, from a bag
All white with flour, the dole of village dames,
He drew his scraps and fragments, one by one ;
And scanned them with a fixed and serious look
Of idle computation.   In the sun,
Upon the second step of that small pile,
Surrounded by those wild unpeopled hills,
He sat, and ate his food in solitude :

And ever, scattered from his palsied hand
That, still attempting to prevent the waste,
Was baffled still, the crumbs in little showers
Fell on the ground ; and the small mountain birds,
Not venturing yet to peck their destined meal,
Approached within the length of half his staff.

Him from my childhood have I known ; and then
He was so old, he seems not older now ;
He travels on, a solitary Man,
So helpless in appearance, that for him
The sauntering Horseman throws not with a slack
And careless hand his alms upon the ground,
But stops,—that he may safely lodge the coin
Within the old Man's hat ; nor quits him so,
But still, when he has given his horse the rein,
Watches the aged Beggar with a look
Sidelong, and half-reverted. She who tends
The toll-gate, when in summer at her door
She turns her wheel, if on the road she sees
The aged Beggar coming, quits her work,
And lifts the latch for him that he may pass.
The post-boy, when his rattling wheels o'ertake
The aged Beggar in the woody lane,
Shouts to him from behind ; and if thus warned
The old man does not change his course, the boy
Turns with less noisy wheels to the roadside,
And passes gently by, without a curse
Upon his lips, or anger at his heart.

He travels on, a solitary Man ;
His age has no companion. On the ground
His eyes are turned, and, as he moves along,

They move along the ground; and, evermore,
Instead of common and habitual sight
Of fields with rural works, of hill and dale,
And the blue sky, one little span of earth
Is all his prospect.   Thus, from day to day,
Bow-bent, his eyes for ever on the ground,
He plies his weary journey; seeing still,
And seldom knowing that he sees, some straw,
Some scattered leaf, or marks which, in one track,
The nails of cart or chariot-wheel have left
Impressed on the white road,—in the same line,
At distance still the same.   Poor Traveller,
His staff trails with him; scarcely do his feet
Disturb the summer dust; he is so still
In look and motion that the cottage curs,
Ere he has passed the door, will turn away,
Weary of barking at him.   Boys and girls,
The vacant and the busy, maids and youths,
And urchins newly breeched—all pass him by:
Him even the slow-paced waggon leaves behind.

But deem not this Man useless.—Statesmen! ye
Who are so restless in your wisdom, ye
Who have a broom still ready in your hands
To rid the world of nuisances; ye proud,
Heart-swoln, while in your pride ye contemplate
Your talents, power, or wisdom, deem him not
A burthen of the earth!   'Tis Nature's law
That none, the meanest of created things,
Of forms created the most vile and brute,
The dullest or most noxious, should exist
Divorced from good—a spirit and pulse of good,
A life and soul, to every mode of being

Inseparably linked.   Then be assured
That least of all can aught—that ever owned
The heaven-regarding eye and front sublime
Which man is born to—sink, howe'er depressed,
So low as to be scorned without a sin ;
Without offence to God cast out of view ;
Like the dry remnant of a garden-flower
Whose seeds are shed, or as an implement
Worn out and worthless.   While from door to door
This old Man creeps, the villagers in him
Behold a record which together binds
Past deeds and offices of charity,
Else unremembered, and so keeps alive
The kindly mood in hearts which lapse of years,
And that half wisdom half experience gives,
Make slow to feel, and by sure steps resign
To selfishness and cold oblivious cares.
Among the farms and solitary huts,
Hamlets and thinly-scattered villages,
Where'er the aged Beggar takes his rounds,
The mild necessity of use compels
To acts of love : and habit does the work
Of reason; yet prepares that after-joy
Which reason cherishes.   And thus the soul,
By that sweet taste of pleasure unpursued,
Doth find herself insensibly disposed
To virtue and true goodness.
                              Some there are,
By their good works exalted, lofty minds
And meditative, authors of delight
And happiness, which to the end of time
Will live, and spread, and kindle : even such minds
In childhood, from the solitary Being,

Or from like wanderer, haply have received
(A thing more precious far than all that books
Or the solicitudes of love can do !)
That first mild touch of sympathy and thought,
In which they found their kindred with a world
Where want and sorrow were.   The easy man
Who sits at his own door,—and, like the pear
That overhangs his head from the green wall,
Feeds in the sunshine ; the robust and young,
The prosperous and unthinking, they who live
Sheltered, and flourish in a little grove
Of their own kindred ;—all behold in him
A silent monitor, which on their minds
Must needs impress a transitory thought
Of self-congratulation, to the heart
Of each recalling his peculiar boons.
His charters and exemptions ; and, perchance,
Though he to no one give the fortitude
And circumspection needful to preserve
His present blessings, and to husband up
The respite of the season, he, at least,
And 'tis no vulgar service, makes them felt.

Yet further.—Many, I believe, there are
Who live a life of virtuous decency,
Men who can hear the Decalogue and feel
No self-reproach ; who of the moral law
Established in the land where they abide
Are strict observers ; and not negligent
In acts of love to those with whom they dwell,
Their kindred, and the children of their blood.
Praise be to such, and to their slumbers peace !
—But of the poor man ask, the abject poor ;

Go, and demand of him, if there be here
In this cold abstinence from evil deeds,
And these inevitable charities,
Wherewith to satisfy the human soul?
No—man is dear to man; the poorest poor
Long for some moments in a weary life
When they can know and feel that they have been,
Themselves, the fathers and the dealers out
Of some small blessings; have been kind to such
As needed kindness, for this single cause,
That we have all of us one human heart.
—Such pleasure is to one kind Being known,
My neighbour, when with punctual care, each week,
Duly as Friday comes, though pressed herself
By her own wants, she from her store of meal
Takes one unsparing handful for the scrip
Of this old Mendicant, and from her door
Returning with exhilarated heart,
Sits by her fire, and builds her hope in heaven.

Then let him pass, a blessing on his head!
And while in that vast solitude to which
The tide of things has borne him, he appears
To breathe and live but for himself alone,
Unblamèd, uninjured, let him bear about
The good which the benignant law of Heaven
Has hung around him: and, while life is his,
Still let him prompt the unlettered villagers
To tender offices and pensive thoughts.
—Then let him pass, a blessing on his head!
And, long as he can wander, let him breathe
The freshness of the valleys; let his blood
Struggle with frosty air and winter snows;

And let the chartered wind that sweeps the heath
¡Beat his grey locks against his withered face.
Reverence the hope whose vital anxiousness
Gives the last human interest to his heart.
May never HOUSE, misnamed of INDUSTRY,
Make him a captive !—for that pent-up din,
Those life-consuming sounds that clog the air,
Be his the natural silence of old age !
Let him be free of mountain solitudes :
And have around him, whether heard or not,
The pleasant melody of woodland birds.
Few are his pleasures : if his eyes have now
Been doomed so long to settle upon earth,
That not without some effort they behold
The countenance of the horizontal sun,
Rising or setting, let the light at least
Find a free entrance to their languid orbs.
And let him, *where* and *when* he will, sit down
Beneath the trees, or on a grassy bank
Of highway side, and with the little birds
Share his chance-gathered meal ; and, finally,
As in the eye of Nature he has lived,
So in the eye of Nature let him die !
   1798.

THE SMALL CELANDINE

THERE is a Flower, the Lesser Celandine,
   That shrinks, like many more, from cold and
   rain ;
And, the first moment that the sun may shine,
Bright as the sun himself, 'tis out again !

When hailstones have been falling, swarm on swarm
Or blasts the green field and the trees distrest,
Oft have I seen it muffled up from harm,
In close self-shelter, like a thing at rest.

But lately, one rough day, this flower I passed
And recognised it, though an altered form,
Now standing forth an offering to the blast,
And buffeted at will by rain and storm.

I stopped, and said with inly muttered voice,
' It doth not love the shower, nor seek the cold :
This neither is its courage nor its choice,
But its necessity in being old.

' The sunshine may not cheer it, nor the dew ;
It cannot help itself in its decay ;
Stiff in its members, withered, changed of hue.'
And, in my spleen, I smiled that it was grey.

To be a Prodigal's Favourite—then, worse truth,
A Miser's Pensioner—behold our lot !
O Man, that from thy fair and shining youth
Age might but take the things Youth needed not !

1804.

EPITAPHS AND ELEGIAC PIECES

ELEGIAC STANZAS

SUGGESTED BY A PICTURE OF PEELE CASTLE IN A STORM, PAINTED BY SIR GEORGE BEAUMONT

I WAS thy neighbour once, thou rugged Pile!
  Four summer weeks I dwelt in sight of thee:
I saw thee every day; and all the while
Thy Form was sleeping on a glassy sea.

So pure the sky, so quiet was the air!
So like, so very like, was day to day!
Whene'er I looked, thy image still was there;
It trembled, but it never passed away.

How perfect was the calm! it seemed no sleep:
No mood, which season takes away, or brings:
I could have fancied that the mighty Deep
Was even the gentlest of all gentle things.

Ah! THEN, if mine had been the Painter's hand,
To express what then I saw; and add the gleam,
The light that never was, on sea or land,
The consecration, and the poet's dream;

I would have planted thee, thou hoary Pile,
Amid a world how different from this!
Beside a sea that could not cease to smile;
On tranquil land, beneath a sky of bliss.

Thou shouldst have seemed a treasure-house divine
Of peaceful years; a chronicle of heaven;—
Of all the sunbeams that did ever shine
The very sweetest had to thee been given.

A Picture had it been of lasting ease,
Elysian quiet, without toil or strife;
No motion but the moving tide, a breeze,
Or merely silent Nature's breathing life.

Such, in the fond illusion of my heart,
Such Picture would I at that time have made:
And seen the soul of truth in every part,
A steadfast peace that might not be betrayed.

So once it would have been,—'tis so no more;
I have submitted to a new control:
A power is gone, which nothing can restore;
A deep distress that humanised my soul.

Not for a moment could I now behold
A smiling sea, and be what I have been:
The feeling of my loss will ne'er be old:
This, which I know, I speak with mind serene.

Then, Beaumont, friend! who would have been the
        friend,
If he had lived, of him whom I deplore,
This work of thine I blame not, but commend;
This sea in anger, and that dismal shore.

O 'tis a passionate Work—yet wise and well;
Well chosen is the spirit that is here;
That Hulk which labours in the deadly swell,
This rueful sky, this pageantry of fear!

And this huge Castle, standing here sublime,
I love to see the look with which it braves,
Cased in the unfeeling armour of old time,
The lightning, the fierce wind, and trampling waves.

Farewell, farewell the heart that lives alone,
Housed in a dream, at distance from the Kind!
Such happiness, wherever it be known,
Is to be pitied; for 'tis surely blind.

But welcome fortitude, and patient cheer,
And frequent sights of what is to be borne!
Such sights, or worse, as are before me here—
Not without hope we suffer and we mourn.

   1805.

LINES

Composed at Grasmere, during a walk one Evening, after a stormy
    day, the Author having just read in a Newspaper that the
    dissolution of Mr. Fox was hourly expected.

LOUD is the Vale! the Voice is up
    With which she speaks when storms are gone,
A mighty unison of streams!
Of all her Voices, One!

Loud is the Vale!—this inland Depth
In peace is roaring like the Sea;
Yon star upon the mountain-top
Is listening quietly.

Sad was I, even to pain deprest,
Importunate and heavy load !
The Comforter hath found me here,
Upon this lonely road ;

And many thousands now are sad—
Wait the fulfilment of their fear ;—
For he must die who is their stay,
Their glory disappear.

A Power is passing from the earth
To breathless Nature's dark abyss ;
But when the great and good depart
What is it more than this—

That Man, who is from God sent forth,
Doth yet again to God return ?—
Such ebb and flow must ever be ;
Then wherefore should we mourn ?
    1806.

EXTEMPORE EFFUSION UPON THE DEATH OF JAMES HOGG

WHEN first, descending from the moorlands,
    I saw the Stream of Yarrow glide
Along a bare and open valley,
The Ettrick Shepherd was my guide.

When last along its banks I wandered,
Through groves that had begun to shed
Their golden leaves upon the pathways,
My steps the Border-minstrel led.

The mighty Minstrel breathes no longer,
Mid mouldering ruins low he lies ;
And death upon the braes of Yarrow,
Has closed the Shepherd-poet's eyes :

Nor has the rolling year twice measured,
From sign to sign, its steadfast course,
Since every mortal power of Coleridge
Was frozen at its marvellous source ;

The rapt One, of the godlike forehead,
The heaven-eyed creature sleeps in earth :
And Lamb, the frolic and the gentle,
Has vanished from his lonely hearth.

Like clouds that rake the mountain-summits
Or waves that own no curbing hand,
How fast has brother followed brother,
From sunshine to the sunless land !

Yet I, whose lids from infant slumber
Were earlier raised, remain to hear
A timid voice, that asks in whispers,
'Who next will drop and disappear?'

Our haughty life is crowned with darkness,
Like London with its own black wreath,
On which with thee, O Crabbe! forth-looking,
I gazed from Hampstead's breezy heath.

As if but yesterday departed,
Thou too art gone before ; but why,
O'er ripe fruit seasonably gathered,
Should frail survivors heave a sigh ?

Mourn rather for that holy Spirit,
Sweet as the spring, as ocean deep;
For Her who, ere her summer faded,
Has sunk into a breathless sleep.

No more of old romantic sorrows,
For slaughtered Youth or love-lorn Maid!
With sharper grief is Yarrow smitten,
And Ettrick mourns with her their Poet dead.

Nov. 1835.

ODE

INTIMATIONS OF IMMORTALITY

FROM RECOLLECTIONS OF EARLY CHILDHOOD

" The Child is father of the Man ;
And I could wish my days to be
Bound each to each by natural piety."

THERE was a time when meadow, grove, and
  stream,
The earth, and every common sight,
   To me did seem
  Apparelled in celestial light,
The glory and the freshness of a dream.
It is not now as it hath been of yore ;—
   Turn wheresoe'er I may,
    By night or day,
The things which I have seen I now can see no more.

   The Rainbow comes and goes,
   And lovely is the Rose,
   The Moon doth with delight
Look round her when the heavens are bare ;
   Waters on a starry night
   Are beautiful and fair ;
  The sunshine is a glorious birth ;
  But yet I know, where'er I go,
That there hath passed away a glory from the earth.

Now, while the birds thus sing a joyous song,
    And while the young lambs bound
      As to the tabor's sound,
To me alone there came a thought of grief:
A timely utterance gave the thought relief,
      And I again am strong:
The cataracts blow their trumpets from the steep;
No more shall grief of mine the season wrong;
I hear the Echoes through the mountains throng,
The Winds come to me from the fields of sleep,
      And all the earth is gay;
        Land and sea
    Give themselves up to jollity,
      And with the heart of May
    Doth every Beast keep holiday;—
      Thou Child of Joy,
Shout round me, let me hear thy shouts, thou happy
    Shepherd-boy!

Ye blessed Creatures, I have heard the call
    Ye to each other make; I see
The heavens laugh with you in your jubilee;
    My heart is at your festival,
    My head hath its coronal,
The fulness of your bliss, I feel—I feel it all.
    Oh evil day! if I were sullen
    While Earth herself is adorning,
      This sweet May-morning,
    And the Children are culling
      On every side,
    In a thousand valleys far and wide,
    Fresh flowers; while the sun shines warm,
And the Babe leaps up on his Mother's arm:—

I hear, I hear, with joy I hear!
—But there's a Tree, of many, one,
A single Field which I have looked upon,
Both of them speak of something that is gone:
        The Pansy at my feet
        Doth the same tale repeat:
Whither is fled the visionary gleam?
Where is it now, the glory and the dream?

Our birth is but a sleep and a forgetting:
The Soul that rises with us, our life's Star,
        Hath had elsewhere its setting,
        And cometh from afar:
        Not in entire forgetfulness,
        And not in utter nakedness,
But trailing clouds of glory do we come
        From God, who is our home:
Heaven lies about us in our infancy!
Shades of the prison-house begin to close
        Upon the growing Boy,
But He beholds the light, and whence it flows,
        He sees it in his joy;
The Youth, who daily farther from the east
        Must travel, still is Nature's Priest,
        And by the vision splendid
        Is on his way attended;
At length the Man perceives it die away,
And fade into the light of common day.

Earth fills her lap with pleasures of her own;
Yearnings she hath in her own natural kind,
And even with something of a Mother's mind,

                And no unworthy aim,
            The homely Nurse doth all she can
        To make her Foster-child, her Inmate Man,
                Forget the glories he hath known,
        And that imperial palace whence he came.

        Behold the Child among his new-born blisses,
        A six years' Darling of a pigmy size !
        See, where 'mid work of his own hand he lies,
        Fretted by sallies of his mother's kisses,
        With light upon him from his father's eyes !
        See, at his feet, some little plan or chart,
        Some fragment from his dream of human life,
        Shaped by himself with newly-learned art ;
                A wedding or a festival,
                A mourning or a funeral,
                    And this hath now his heart,
                And unto this he frames his song :
                    Then will he fit his tongue
        To dialogues of business, love, or strife.
                    But it will not be long
                    Ere this be thrown aside,
                    And with new joy and pride
        The little Actor cons another part ;
        Filling from time to time his 'humorous stage !'
        With all the Persons, down to palsied Age,
        That Life brings with her in her equipage ;
                    As if his whole vocation
                    Were endless imitation.

        Thou, whose exterior semblance doth belie
                    Thy Soul's immensity ;

Thou best Philosopher, who yet dost keep
Thy heritage, thou Eye among the blind,
That, deaf and silent, read'st the eternal deep,
Haunted for ever by the external mind,—
        Mighty Prophet! Seer blest!
        On whom those truths do rest,
Which we are toiling all our lives to find,
In darkness lost, the darkness of the grave;
Thou, over whom thy Immortality
Broods like the Day, a Master o'er a Slave
A Presence which is not to be put by;
Thou little Child, yet glorious in the might
Of heaven-born freedom on thy being's height,
Why with such earnest pains dost thou provoke
The years to bring the inevitable yoke,
Thus blindly with thy blessedness at strife?
Full soon thy Soul shall have her earthly freight,
And custom lie upon thee with a weight,
Heavy as frost, and deep almost as life!

        O joy! that in our embers
        Is something that doth live,
        That Nature yet remembers
        What was so fugitive!
The thought of our past years in me doth breed
Perpetual benediction : not indeed
For that which is most worthy to be blest;
Delight and liberty, the simple creed
Of Childhood, whether busy or at rest,
With new-fledged hope still fluttering in his breast:—
        Not for these I raise
        The song of thanks and praise;

But for those obstinate questionings
Of sense and outward things,
Fallings from us, vanishings;
Blank misgivings of a Creature
Moving about in worlds not realised,
High instincts before which our mortal Nature
Did tremble like a guilty thing surprised:
But for those first affections,
Those shadowy recollections,
Which, be they what they may,
Are yet the fountain light of all our day,
Are yet a master light of all our seeing;
Uphold us, cherish, and have power to make
Our noisy years seem moments in the being
Of the eternal Silence: truths that wake,
To perish never;
Which neither listlessness, nor mad endeavour,
Nor Man nor Boy,
Nor all that is at enmity with joy,
Can utterly abolish or destroy!
Hence, in a season of calm weather,
Though inland far we be,
Our souls have sight of that immortal sea
Which brought us hither,
Can in a moment travel thither,
And see the Children sport upon the shore,
And hear the mighty waters rolling evermore.

Then sing, ye Birds, sing, sing a joyous song!
And let the young Lambs bound
As to the tabor's sound!
We in thought will join your throng,

Ye that pipe and ye that play,
Ye that through your hearts to-day
Feel the gladness of the May !
What though the radiance which was once so
    bright
Be now for ever taken from my sight,
    Though nothing can bring back the hour
Of splendour in the grass, of glory in the flower ;
    We will grieve not, rather find
    Strength in what remains behind ;
    In the primal sympathy
    Which having been must ever be ;
    In the soothing thoughts that spring
    Out of human suffering ;
    In the faith that looks through death,
In years that bring the philosophic mind.

And oh, ye Fountains, Meadows, Hills, and
    Groves,
Forebode not any severing of our loves !
Yet in my heart of hearts I feel your might ;
I only have relinquished one delight
To live beneath your more habitual sway.
I love the Brooks which down their channels
    fret,
Even more than when I tripped lightly as they ;
The innocent brightness of a new-born Day
        Is lovely yet ;
The Clouds that gather round the setting sun
Do take a sober colouring from an eye
That hath kept watch o'er man's mortality ;
Another race hath been, and other palms are
    won.

Thanks to the human heart by which we live,
Thanks to its tenderness, its joys, and fears,
To me the meanest flower that blows can give
Thoughts that do often lie too deep for tears.
1803–6.

PENGUIN POPULAR CLASSICS

Published or forthcoming

Aesop	Aesop's Fables
Hans Andersen	Fairy Tales
Louisa May Alcott	Good Wives
	Little Women
Eleanor Atkinson	Greyfriars Bobby
Jane Austen	Emma
	Mansfield Park
	Northanger Abbey
	Persuasion
	Pride and Prejudice
	Sense and Sensibility
R. M. Ballantyne	The Coral Island
J. M. Barrie	Peter Pan
Frank L. Baum	The Wonderful Wizard of Oz
Anne Brontë	Agnes Grey
	The Tenant of Wildfell Hall
Charlotte Brontë	Jane Eyre
	The Professor
	Shirley
	Villette
Emily Brontë	Wuthering Heights
John Buchan	Greenmantle
	The Thirty-Nine Steps
Frances Hodgson Burnett	A Little Princess
	Little Lord Fauntleroy
	The Secret Garden
Samuel Butler	The Way of All Flesh
Lewis Carroll	Alice's Adventures in Wonderland
	Through the Looking Glass
Geoffrey Chaucer	The Canterbury Tales
G. K. Chesterton	Father Brown Stories
Erskine Childers	The Riddle of the Sands
John Cleland	Fanny Hill
Wilkie Collins	The Moonstone
	The Woman in White
Sir Arthur Conan Doyle	The Adventures of Sherlock Holmes
	His Last Bow
	The Hound of the Baskervilles

PENGUIN POPULAR CLASSICS

Published or forthcoming

Joseph Conrad	Heart of Darkness
	Lord Jim
	Nostromo
	The Secret Agent
	Victory
James Fenimore Cooper	The Last of the Mohicans
Stephen Crane	The Red Badge of Courage
Daniel Defoe	Moll Flanders
	Robinson Crusoe
Charles Dickens	Bleak House
	The Christmas Books
	David Copperfield
	Great Expectations
	Hard Times
	Little Dorrit
	Martin Chuzzlewit
	Nicholas Nickleby
	The Old Curiosity Shop
	Oliver Twist
	The Pickwick Papers
	A Tale of Two Cities
Fyodor Dostoyevsky	Crime and Punishment
George Eliot	Adam Bede
	Middlemarch
	The Mill on the Floss
	Silas Marner
John Meade Falkner	Moonfleet
Henry Fielding	Tom Jones
F. Scott Fitzgerald	The Diamond as Big as the Ritz
	The Great Gatsby
	Tender is the Night
Gustave Flaubert	Madame Bovary
Elizabeth Gaskell	Cousin Phillis
	Cranford
	Mary Barton
	North and South
Kenneth Grahame	The Wind in the Willows

PENGUIN POPULAR CLASSICS

Published or forthcoming

George Grossmith	The Diary of a Nobody
Brothers Grimm	Grimm's Fairy Tales
H. Rider Haggard	Allan Quatermain
	King Solomon's Mines
Thomas Hardy	Far from the Madding Crowd
	Jude the Obscure
	The Mayor of Casterbridge
	A Pair of Blue Eyes
	The Return of the Native
	Tess of the D'Urbervilles
	The Trumpet-Major
	Under the Greenwood Tree
	The Woodlanders
Nathaniel Hawthorne	The Scarlet Letter
Anthony Hope	The Prisoner of Zenda
Thomas Hughes	Tom Brown's Schooldays
Victor Hugo	The Hunchback of Notre-Dame
Henry James	The Ambassadors
	The American
	The Aspern Papers
	Daisy Miller
	The Europeans
	The Portrait of a Lady
	The Turn of the Screw
	Washington Square
M. R. James	Ghost Stories
Jerome K. Jerome	Three Men in a Boat
	Three Men on the Bummel
James Joyce	Dubliners
	A Portrait of the Artist as a Young Man
Charles Kingsley	The Water Babies
Rudyard Kipling	Captains Courageous
	The Jungle Books
	Just So Stories
	Kim
	Plain Tales from the Hills
	Puck of Pook's Hill

PENGUIN POPULAR CLASSICS

Published or forthcoming

Charles and Mary Lamb	Tales from Shakespeare
D. H. Lawrence	Lady Chatterley's Lover
	The Rainbow
	Sons and Lovers
	Women in Love
Edward Lear	Book of Nonsense
Gaston Leroux	The Phantom of the Opera
Jack London	White Fang *and* The Call of the Wild
Captain Marryat	The Children of the New Forest
Guy de Maupassant	Selected Short Stories
Herman Melville	Billy Budd, Sailor
	Moby-Dick
John Milton	Paradise Lost
Edith Nesbit	The Railway Children
Edgar Allan Poe	Selected Tales
	Spirits of the Dead
Thomas de Quincey	Confessions of an English Opium Eater
Damon Runyon	Guys and Dolls
Sir Walter Scott	Ivanhoe
	Rob Roy
	Waverley
Saki	The Best of Saki
William Shakespeare	Antony and Cleopatra
	As You Like It
	Hamlet
	Henry V
	Julius Caesar
	King Lear
	Macbeth
	Measure for Measure
	The Merchant of Venice
	A Midsummer Night's Dream
	Much Ado About Nothing
	Othello
	Romeo and Juliet
	The Tempest
	Twelfth Night

PENGUIN POPULAR CLASSICS

Published or forthcoming

Anna Sewell	Black Beauty
Mary Shelley	Frankenstein
Johanna Spyri	Heidi
Robert Louis Stevenson	The Black Arrow
	A Child's Garden of Verses
	Dr Jekyll and Mr Hyde
	Kidnapped
	Treasure Island
Bram Stoker	Dracula
Jonathan Swift	Gulliver's Travels
W. M. Thackeray	Vanity Fair
Leo Tolstoy	War and Peace
Anthony Trollope	Barchester Towers
	Framley Parsonage
	The Small House at Allington
	The Warden
Mark Twain	The Adventures of Huckleberry Finn
	The Adventures of Tom Sawyer
	The Prince and the Pauper
Vatsyayana	The Kama Sutra
Jules Verne	Around the World in Eighty Days
	Journey to the Centre of the Earth
	Twenty Thousand Leagues under the Sea
Voltaire	Candide
Edith Wharton	The Age of Innocence
	Ethan Frome
Oscar Wilde	The Happy Prince and Other Stories
	The Importance of Being Earnest
	Lady Windermere's Fan
	Lord Arthur Savile's Crime
	The Picture of Dorian Gray
	A Woman of No Importance
Virginia Woolf	Mrs Dalloway
	Orlando
	To the Lighthouse

PENGUIN POPULAR POETRY

Published or forthcoming

The Selected Poems *of:*

Matthew Arnold
William Blake
Robert Browning
Robert Burns
Lord Byron
John Donne
Thomas Hardy
John Keats
Rudyard Kipling
Alexander Pope
Alfred Tennyson
William Wordsworth
William Yeats

and collections of:

Seventeenth-Century Poetry
Eighteenth-Century Poetry
Poetry of the Romantics
Victorian Poetry
Twentieth-Century Poetry
Scottish Folk and Fairy Tales